99 Theses:

Disputations on the Power, Efficacy, and Indulgences of the United States Government, Businesses, and Other Institutions

Table of Contents

16. Improve Food Safety And Nutrition

17. Fortify National Food Security

18. Abolish Factory Farms

19. Destroy "Big Food" Monopolies

20. Make All School Lunches Free

21. Create Universal Nutrition Accessibility

Medical

22. Enact Universal Healthcare

23. Create Mental Health Infrastructure

24. Stop Diagnosing Natural Childhood Behaviors As Disorders

25. Implement Stronger Vaccination Policies

26. Allow Universal Access To Contraception

27. Protect Women's Bodily Autonomy

28. Destroy "Big Pharma"

Civil Rights

29. Make Election A National Holiday

30. Rein In Eminent Domain

31. Protect Marriage Equality

32. End Racist And Sexist Pay Gaps

33. End The "Pink Tax"

34. Ban Gay Conversion Therapy

35. Recognize LGBTQ Rights As Human Rights

36. Fight Obesity Discrimination

37. End Violence Against Protestors

38. Stop Arresting Protestors

39. End Mass Surveillance

40. Repeal The Patriot Act

41. Eliminate "Black Sites"

42. Justice For The Tortured

Law Enforcement

43. Repeal Restrictive "Off-Grid" Laws

44. Legalize Prostitution

45. Legalize Cannabis

46. Decriminalize All Drug Use

47. End Police Quotas

48. Stop Literal Over-Policing

49. Stop Policing For Profit

50. Cease The Reemergence Of Debtor Prisons

51. Abolish For-Profit Private Prisons

52. Abolish For-Profit Private Law Firms

53. Stop Indiscriminate Use Of "Non-Lethal" Weapons

54. Create Accountability For Police Officers

55. End And Reverse Police Militarization

56. Forbid The Use Of Advanced Surveillance Technologies

57. End Racist Sentencing

58. Implement Criminal Justice Reform

59. Improve Prison Quality

60. Abolish The Death Penalty

Government

61. Encourage Community

62. Reform The Legislative Process

63. Require Subject Literacy In Congress

64. Eliminate Big Money In Politics

65. Break The Revolving Door

66. Improve The Accuracy Of Our Representation

67. Abolish The Electoral College

68. Enact Austerity Measures For Congress

69. Increase Veterans Benefits

70. Relax Voter ID Laws

71. Overhaul The Immigration System

72. Abolish ICE

73. Enact Common Sense Gun Control Legislation

74. Create Term Limits For Judges

75. Respect Sovereignty Of Tribal Nations

76. Reduce Defense Spending

77. End Drone Programs

78. Stop Endless, Illegal Regime Change Wars

79. Hold Administrations Accountable For War Crimes

80. Disarm Nuclear Stockpiles

81. Demand Disclosure

Economy And Wealth Inequality

82. End Initial Job Applications Asking About Convictions

83. Forgive Student Loan Debt

84. Fund Social Safety Nets

85. Make Minimum Wage A Thriving Wage

86. End Homelessness And Its Criminalization

87. Implement Universal Basic Income

88. Implement Universal Basic Assets

89. Legally Differentiate Between Corporations And People

90. Create A New Tax Code

91. Raise Top Marginal Tax Bracket Rates

92. Tax Wealth And Assets

93. Tax Churches

94. End Corporate Welfare

95. Arrest Those Responsible For The 2008 Financial Crisis

96. Regulate Finance Industries

Introduction

The 2008 financial crises, when we all witnessed incompetent or predatory executives who run their businesses and the global economy into the ground receive bailouts and bonuses while ordinary people lost their jobs and homes, precipitated the Occupy Wall Street movement only a few years later. While not the only catalyst for the movement, the Great Recession remains the most obvious and well known example responsible for instigating the protests. The numbers and data illustrating the extent of financial inequalities in the United States and the world as a whole were for many literally unbelievable. Despite increased productivity and profits 99% of the population saw no real improvement in the financial stability, upward mobility, wages, or benefits. Instead, decades worth of increasing profits poured into the bank accounts of the now infamous 1%.

Mainstream media quickly dismissed many of the issues highlighted by activists and protestors with one of their chief criticisms being that OWS wasn't about anything at all because it was about so many things and therefore everyone involved had no real issues to be complaining about other than their own bad life choices. Although the movement faded from the spotlight it still continues today in the form of localized community groups with various priorities and missions across the country. The problems responsible for triggering the wave of mass protest continue and along with a host of other problems have steadily worsened since. Wealth and income inequality are still increasing; people are still dying of treatable illnesses because they can't afford their medications; we have been at war for almost two decades; the climate is changing before our eyes; we are locking children in concentration camps; and the list continues at length.

The following are brief summations of various, often similar and interconnected issues along with suggestions for addressing them. Issues are organized into several categories: education; media and technology; energy; food and nutrition; medical; civil rights; law enforcement; government; and economy and wealth inequality. This is not a comprehensive list of all our problems, but they are arguably the most pressing. The suggested courses of action are likewise only starting points that will hopefully inspire others to come up with new creative solutions. Though the number of issues and their severity may seem overwhelming, if we picked just one to personally focus on and we all picked an issue to focus on we can make the world a better place. We can change the future. And we must.

Education

1 - Implement Holistic Education

The United States routinely scores near the bottom when compared to other developed nations in all areas of learning. Intelligence is often mocked instead of praised and we have become obsessed with testing instead of teaching students. In fact, the entire design from K-12 schooling is an antiquated factory model intended to churn out as many obedient workers who are intelligent enough to operate machinery. This design asphyxiates creativity, deprives our country and humanity of talent located outside traditional pedantic standards.

We must move away from the factory model and towards something that gives each individual child the resources to fulfil their potential; evolve our methods of teaching students so they align with psychological insights of different learning styles. An emphasis should be placed more on thinking as opposed to regurgitation of facts. Facts alone without context and without a student's ability to think critically and understand the importance and implications of those facts impedes a student's ability to gain any real, applicable knowledge as well as leaving the bigger picture of any subject obscured.

At present the US education system uses the transmission model of education which sees education as something that is transmitted from teacher to student. Its methods are typically rote rehearsal and memorization. However, alternative methods and models of education already exist: freedom-based learning, which emphasizes the students' desires and interests; social constructivist which views education as something requiring social interaction; critical pedagogy sees education as a means to the goal of bettering the world and its communities, and holistic which includes its own set of values while also recognizing the value in the other models. Several others models exist along with numerous methods that can be mixed and matched from each teaching style.

Perhaps most obviously, instead of allowing various mandated tests to consume so much time and effort from both teachers and students let's get back to having teachers teaching and students learning. Many teachers will attest to the drawbacks of such testing including the flaws both in design and implementation. While all students in a certain grade must take the same test, students with learning disabilities for example may not be afforded the proper accommodations to perform as well as they potentially could.

And perhaps most importantly, our culture must also change so intelligence is praised and not mocked. It must change also the way students with atypical learning modes are viewed and incorporate them more fully into the curriculum. Without a child's desire to learn they likely won't. If they're going to be bullied for being a "nerd," or "teacher's pet," or subjected to any of the far crueler things children do to one another; if there is no value in knowledge beyond the classroom; if there's no one willing to teach them in a way they'll understand why would a child feel safe enough, or a desire to learn?

2 - Improve Education Culture

American public schools are where we teach children how to be future prisoners. Public schools face a number of other problems too including a declining quality of education, deteriorating facilities, overcrowding, low quality food, and increasing violence. More and more schools are installing metal detectors as the number of school shootings keeps rising; entrances with electronic doors requiring a student ID card for entry; a permanent police presence on school grounds – which has done nothing but embolden the School-to-Prison Pipeline; and camera installations all the while students need to share books and there's mold growing on the ceiling.

The quality of food is also deplorable, often bought at discount prices because the food has received the lowest rating by the USDA. Some schools have gone so far as to ban junk foods, sodas, chocolate milk, peanut butter and even lunches prepared at home for various reasons. It seems as though schools are increasingly prison like, but with worse food.

Zero tolerance policies have failed at best and backfired at worst. Children are suspended for the most trivial matters when a reprimand, or detention, would be sufficient. Students have been arrested for offenses of the same nature. Both suspension and, obviously, an arrest are detrimental to a student's learning and do nothing to mollify negative behaviors. Environments like this are not conducive to learning except for learning that it's normal to be watched all the time and to feel criminalized.

It's not just more serious behavioral zero tolerance policies have failed, so have food restrictions. Schools that banned soda and junk foods saw students bringing them in from home and selling them to other students. When chocolate milk was banned in at least one instance, milk sales simply stopped meaning the children were getting absolutely none of the benefits of drinking milk. A school that bans homemade lunches puts more of a financial burden on low income families to pay for school lunches every day.

The biggest difference between schools and actual prisons is that prisoners often receive all the benefits of schools without any of the costs. Depending on the type of prison, prisoners are allowed yard time (recess), three meals a day (better than just breakfast and lunch), have access to libraries and education programs so they may be better able to find a job when released; in some cases they even receive help finding housing, further education, job training, and job placement which is actually more than schools provide. These amenities are free for the prisoners; they're paid for with taxes. Why can't we do at least as much for students?

But how can violence, the quality of education, and food quality, all, be addressed? Schools could actually adapt some methods from prisons for psychologically deterring violence. Less crowded schools would probably result in less tension between students and thus less conflict. Better access to councilors may also provide relief in the effort to deter violence in schools.

The quality of education can be improved in part by fixing the first two problems: a less stressful and less violence prone environment along with better food will result in healthier, less stressed students who can then focus on school work and doing what children do: socializing, participating in sports, and other school programs and functions which overall will lead to a better quality of education and better quality of experience. The problem is too often cuts are made to save money at the expense of children's education and our future.

Another crucial aspect for bettering education is in regards to maintaining democracy: informed citizens are a necessity. However, with the advent of the Internet, twenty-four hour news networks, and social media the amount of information thrust at us is overwhelming and growing. And education is the best tool in our disposal for combatting propaganda and fake news. The ability to critically evaluate sources is more important for day-to-day life than it's ever been before. Having a framework for critical thinking is difficult to encourage and made even more so by a lack of education funding and resources.

More funding is required to lessen crowding by building new schools. Funding is required for better food. Funding is required for better consoler and mental health access. And at the same time strict polices should be loosened so students don't feel like their being treated like criminals. Where would this funding come from? There exists no shortage in cash flow, just a shortage of political will to allocate it properly. Alternatively, taxes could be increased; businesses could donate money, or be required to pay higher taxes especially if they're making billions each year. And this funding is not a waste of money, or a handout, but an investment. Better education means more successful students who in turn are more successful workers and thus produce a more robust economy. Deeper than that, education should be treated as a means to its own ends and not only as a right, not only an investment, but a public good- which it truly is.

3 - Teach Comprehensive Sexual Education

People are born with innate sexual urges, but they are not born with the knowledge of how to properly act on those urges. Sex and sexuality are complicated, nuanced subjects that touch all of our lives and yet as children become young adults they are often woefully unaware of even basic reproductive anatomy let alone how to properly utilize various birth control methods or protect themselves from STI's. We have no national standards for a subject that relates to literally everybody so no two school districts are necessarily teaching the same information. Furthermore, abstinence only curriculums are not real curriculums at all and leave young people ignorant and vulnerable.

We require a national comprehensive sexual education curriculum that covers everything from basic reproductive health to communication and consent. School districts that have more rigorous sex-ed classes experience lower rates of high school pregnancies along with correspondingly lower dropout rates and reported cases of STI's. Understanding ourselves and our bodies is a necessity for both our physical and mental wellbeing.

4 - Teach Non-Whitewashed History

From grade school through university studies the version of history being taught is all too often inaccurate and whitewashed. For example, textbooks in some states refer to slaves as "involuntary immigrants," portray the Civil War as being about the South's righteous struggle to uphold their way of life and to defend State's rights. While the Civil War was indeed fought over State's rights and to preserve the Southern way of life certain popular text books fail to complete those sentences: the Civil War was fought on behalf of the South to defend a State's right to use slavery and to preserve the Southern way of life built upon chattel slavery. American History classes also focus on battles, dates, and generals far more than the human cost and impacts still reverberating today. Another obvious and more pervasive example is Black History Month: we dedicate the shortest month of year to focus on the contributions of important black historical figures, but history is inseparable from "black history." US history is especially inseparable because it was built on the backs of black slaves and the continuing oppression of non-white populations. The historical narrative being taught is meant to instill national pride and serves as propaganda. In an effort to create patriotism we focus almost exclusively on white historical figures while ignoring US atrocities and have created a crisis dooming us to repeat our mistakes.

An understanding of history is important to a national sense of identity and for understanding how we got to where we are. It's crucial to be able to recognize mistakes and learn from them. We need to create a new curriculum that includes the story non-white populations within the overall narrative. A better and more accurate understanding of history would also make us more understanding of each other.

5 - End School Funding Inequality

Funding public schools through property taxes maintains and enlarges the gap between rich and poor through each generation. Because public schools are primarily funded by local and state taxes there's a disparity in educational resources between the states and even between school districts within the same state. A disparity in funding and resources results in a disparity between achievement levels. The wealth and income gaps are exacerbated by this unequal school funding because more affluent districts will produce more successful students who in turn earn more than their counterparts educated in less affluent districts.

Quality education is a necessity for a healthy democracy and a healthy economy, to say nothing of a healthy mind. Arguably, quality education is a human right and shouldn't only be accessible to the wealthy. Without proper education upward social mobility becomes harder to achieve and this current funding method undermines the futures of students based solely on where they live while maintaining the truth of the phrase "the rich get richer and poor stay poor." More problems arise when national and state testing are concerned; instead of accurately portraying how well students and schools are performing it is in essence measuring the performance between affluent and underfunded schools.

What can be done to make schools not only more equitable, but more proficient? Simply taking money from school districts that can afford more money per student and reallocating it to poorer school districts would only lead to equal mediocrity by helping the poorer districts by hurting the wealthier ones. That can't be the way and just as students in low income areas shouldn't have their education suffer, neither should the students in affluent areas. No one deserves to have their education cut in quality. More federal funding could certainly be cut from military spending and given to schools. But, not all schools would receive the same amount of money. Instead a national standard could be set for money spent per student. Schools would then be given the amount needed to meet that standard. Some schools may still be funded enough through local and state taxes to have more than that amount, but no one would be left with less than the new standard.

This investment would lead to more successful students who then become more successful workers who will in turn drive the economy forward by securing better jobs and spending more. An investment in education is an investment in the most important resource of any nation: its human capital. These students will go on to create new, innovative solutions to old problems. They'll be better informed about the world around them and more informed about events within the US, hopefully leading to better voter turnout and healthier elections.

6 - Pay College Students

The cost of higher education has risen, and is still rising, at a meteoric pace that far outruns inflation making it harder to attain especially for low income families. Historically, education has been something for the elites: the wealthy, the nobility, etc. But this is the United States in the 21st century. Unfortunately, we have already largely regressed to this outdated mode where education increasingly something only for the wealthy. The current generation is already straddled with massive college debt and future generations of prospective students know this. The next generation will likely reject the financial risk of a college education altogether. Looming college debt has already led to problems with the economy and the overall quality of life for tens of millions of Americans with no solutions, or relief in sight.

When only the wealthy are able to attain higher education then only the wealthy will maintain the positions that allow wealth to be created. Already, there exists a large population of surplus labor enabling businesses to keep wages low because somebody's always poor and desperate enough to work whenever current employees burn out, or quit. As education decreases in its accessibility the undereducated will increasingly flood the bottom of job market with even more surplus labor. And, despite what CEO's might think, this helps nobody, not even themselves, because if the majority of Americans are struggling to pay for essentials, they will not be spending money on other things like new cars, houses, televisions, computers, or any other non-essential products. The owners of many companies will begin making less because no one can afford to buy what they make. This may lead to even fewer jobs being available which will only compound the problem further.

Living costs have increased. The price of a diploma has increased while its value has decreased as has the average salary accompanying said diploma. And often more advanced (and expensive) schooling is required for students to enter their desired field. Students are often mocked when picking a non-business, or non-STEM, major because our society does not truly value the humanities, arts, or education for their own sakes, but because of this stigma and devaluation other fields are oversaturated making employment competitive and difficult to find.

The solution may be to follow the lead of some European nations which have various means of paying for higher education. Some countries like Germany and Finland have free tuition for all students. Others not only have free tuition, but provide students with money so they can live without being forced to work the entire time they're in school, thus allowing them to better focus on their studies, and presumably also saving them some sanity and stress. This money could from different sources at state and federal levels. If the US can afford to build multi-million dollar fighter jets and stealth aircraft en masse, it can afford to invest in its own future via higher education for all who want it.

Media And Technology

7 - Demand Informative Journalism

Schools, colleges, and universities are not the only places we're supposed to learn from; we're also supposed to learn from the Fourth Estate: the free press. Unfortunately, we have megalithic institutions of news and journalism that compete for attention instead of accuracy while pushing their own bias and establishment talking points.

We have twenty-four hour news networks, online news, full length documentaries, and print media. Unfortunately these sources sensationalize unimportant stories, under report important stories, report untrue facts often without correction, or devote more time to celebrity scandals than the latest developments in politics and world affairs. This is why "Last Week Tonight" and "The Daily Show,"-whose tagline is "The Real Fake News"- are considered by younger generations to be more "real news" than what's supposed to be the "real news?" While sensationalism and petty stories about internet memes may never go away, nor necessarily should they, these stories should not be the focus of any major network except on channels devoted to entertainment and diversions already. Twenty-four hours every day of the week is a lot of time to fill, but the quality of the news suffers, perhaps because of the quantity, but quantity can't replace quality. Even many so called "documentaries" have false information and possess claims already debunked.

Our Fourth Estate could learn something themselves from the presentation of news portrayed on shows like the "Daily Show" and "Last Week Tonight." News networks would not have to be as extreme, or crass, as these shows can be, but humor that pokes fun at all sides of an issue could draw and keep an audience. More importantly they highlight the absurdity and ridiculousness of the stories they cover. News networks must, and we must demand of them, to fact check themselves and other networks, stop taking clips and quotes out of context, focus on the important stories more often than not, and eliminate as much bias as possible. And if they can't find the time with their twenty-four hour schedules to report honestly with quality, maybe they should consider cutting some hours from the constant flow of minutia we currently consider news. We must also demand an end to the megalithic nature of these institutions. They coalesced into larger and larger conglomerates until now only six giants control all of our media and can easily influence the flow of information. They need to be litigated out of existence and can be done so under extant antitrust laws.

8 - Hold Journalists And Institutions Accountable For Accuracy

The problems mentioned above with modern media have many sources ranging from monopolistic concerns to major unaccountability issues. Despite being a comedy show, the "real news" would on occasion call out the previous host, Jon Stewart, for getting facts incorrect and every time Stewart owned it. He corrected himself, set the record straight, and moved on. The mainstream media outlets do retract and correct false information, but not as often as they should, perhaps having more false than true information being purported as news.

Most outlets have a bias whether it's conservative, or liberal, and we viewers will tend to watch the networks that coincide with our own views thus limiting our perspectives and information. News anchors, networks and all forms of media must be held accountable for purporting false information as truth with perhaps only one exception: during live developing news stories like 9/11 or the Boston Marathon Bombing; it's difficult to have all the facts as such events unfold. After the events have concluded, and as more information becomes available, the previous live reports should nonetheless be corrected. But how can media outlets be held accountable and what if any punishment should be given? They cannot be held responsible by the government, for not only can there be no laws restricting the news and freedom of speech via Constitutional rights, but it could, and probably would, be a slippery slope from corrections to censorship.

Solutions are available and to some are already to some extent apart of journalistic institutions. An individual person, or network, first should self-correct, but we cannot and should not rely on just someone's word alone. Other stations should report and call out other stations which they do to some extent already, but should be done more intently. Independent organizations which already exist and fact check statements by politicians and the media at large must become more widely known and that burden lies mostly with us to check our sources. However it's extremely difficult to fact check every story and every claim especially with contradictory accounts and multiple twenty-four hour news stations. So how can we keep up with the news and trust that it's accurate? We should never entirely trust the news and rather view it with an open mind.

Perhaps, another way to keep the media honest is have them incur some form of punishment for unrepentant, uncorrected, and consistent falsification of the truth either for purposeful misleading, or incompetence. People should first be fired or forced to resign for consistent errors. Sponsors who purchase ad time should pull their ads. And perhaps for the worst and most consistent offender fines could levied against them and the fines could go to charity. An independent fact checker should not be the one to receive or levy such fines because it creates an incentive to falsify facts in the fact checking process, or to be too strict in fining news organizations to the point of making reporters afraid to report out of fear of accidentally getting even some minute bit of information wrong. This institution could be a sort of Supreme Court for journalism which forces small mistakes to be corrected and major and consistent mistakes penalized.

It may seem extreme the suggestions above, but for some individuals it may not be sufficient. If an anchor, network executive, or whomever knowingly spreads false and damaging information as fact and en mass they should be sentenced to prison for some extended period of time. Demonstrably false claims of a personal nature can ruin someone's livelihood, their marriage, and their entire lives. Similarly false stories peddled as truth in the mainstream media can play an important role in going to war, the outcome of elections, and the resurgence of diseases thought eradicated. These and other forms of malicious deception have real consequences that cost lives and the people responsible for the propagation of false information should be held accountable for their actions.

9 - Recognize Internet Access As A Public Utility

The Internet is now so embedded within our society it truly should be considered a public utility. It's often necessary for people to communicate with their employers, employees, customers, clients, and of course family and friends via email, video conferences, or virtual reality forums. It's a medium for news and advertising too. It can be used to pay bills, check bank statements, and many businesses won't even accept physical applications anymore, instead requiring applicants to file online. The Internet is now an integral part of our lives. It is a source of education and so much more.

However, there are those who would prefer to not have the Internet classified as a utility, despite its literal utility. Some would still like to censor the Internet through privatization. With the destruction of net-neutrality Internet providers can change speeds of specific sites for whatever reasons they choose like giving affiliated companies and sites better speed; or slowing down competitors; or extorting money from clients by slowing down browser, or individual site speeds unless clients pay more. Instead of everyone getting the same speed and ease of access we have a deregulated industry that the entire modern world is built around that can now legally manipulate its own marketplace at the expense of customers.

Internet Providers can also potentially further facilitate their partnerships with government agencies by slowing down connection speeds to sites the government declares inappropriate. Destroying net neutrality further unevened the playing field that gives those with wealth even more of an unfair and unneeded advantage. Whenever unscrupulous business practices arise which would restrict these matters we must demand our representatives take action to prevent said bills from passing and ban said business practices. If they continually fail to listen we should demand and force their resignation. The Internet needs to be open, uncensored, and neutral. To allow anything else infringes upon free speech and will lead to censorship.

10 - Limit Auto-Customization Search Filters

The Internet, or more accurately our experience of the Internet, is a personalized one; everything from search engines, news sites, and social media sites are algorithmically fine-tuning our content. The official reason for this is simply to give users easier access to things they want and are interested in which compels users to keep coming back. It's a matter of convenience intended to make user experiences better and customized to our tastes. But, there are "unintended" consequences. This personalization limits what we see and even changes our general search results from person to person. We see fewer and fewer opposing viewpoints creating a personalized bubble of perception for each person. This digital bubble ultimately makes us more ignorant of important issues while reinforcing our current views and preconceived notions instead of challenging them; presenting new evidence which may contradict, or even disprove, our personal beliefs; and then updating our beliefs as necessary.

The Internet is not just a source of entertainment, but is a source of education and a way to engage with the entire world. This can't happen if it's overly tailored to individuals giving different people different information. It has the potential to divide us further apart instead of educating everyone with the same important information. We should first check our own filter settings if they exist and then petition the sites we use to at least give us the option to choose if we get personalized results, and not have the feature buried under numerous option tabs if accessible at all. If they cannot do that, they should just not do customization at all.

11 - End Planned Obsolescence

The tech companies responsible for creating the devices embedded into our daily lives rely on rare, non-renewable metals which are difficult and environmentally destructive to extract. Tech companies also build obsolesce into their devices ensuring we need to keep buying new ones. Cell phones become unusable after so many software updates despite remaining physically fine. Various features for personal computers could merely be replaced and upgraded if companies did not purposely make them different shapes rendering different models incompatible.

Planned obsolesce cannot be permitted to continue. Technology manufacturers must be regulated into making all models and software as upgradable and user friendly as possible. Furthermore, electronic devices must be safely recycled and their raw materials reused less we run out of materials to continually make new devices. People must also be permitted the right to work and modify their own property enabling anyone and everyone to work on their own machines.

Energy

12 - Stop Using Fossil Fuels

Reliance on fossil fuels to power the bulk of modern civilization is completely absurd. The facts as we know them: fossil fuels are limited and will run out; the emissions and byproducts from using them harm the environment immensely by polluting the air, water, and land which are obviously all very important for life to continue living; and they are the paramount reason for climate change which now threatens the human race as a species. "The Flintstones" had a more sustainable way of life and energy. However, the government continues to subsidize fossil fuels and their production. Oil companies receive billions of dollars annually to keep prices lower. And oil companies lobby Congress to pass laws in their favor and keep the subsidies coming. The US openly supports and instigates coups and regime changes in sovereign nations around the world to control their oil. This cannot continue.

Fracking is another form of extracting dangerous fossil fuels from the earth at the expense of environment and human health. It's an environmentally destructive process by which water is pumped into the ground creating pressure that forces natural gases to the surface. Proponents of the extraction process contend it makes us more energy independent and creates jobs. However, the jobs created are hazardous and made more so by lax safety enforcement and deregulation. Fracking workers are sustaining serious injuries and occasionally dying on the job followed by little if any compensation. The environmental impacts of fracking far outweigh any contributions towards energy independence: it's responsible for contaminating local water supplies with flammable gasses and even create geological instability resulting in more frequent seismic activity. Retrieving natural gas also uses an exorbitant amount of resources like water and carcinogenic chemicals. It's economic benefit is too little for the human cost and should be prohibited, just compensation paid to injured workers and families of deceased works, and fracking companies must be required to pay restitution to undue all the environmental damage cause in the name of profit.

At present we must switch from using fossil fuels to other sustainable forms of energy and prohibit any new extraction proceedings along with strict limitations on burning reserves. While their usage is a cornerstone of modern life powering everything from cities to our cars, planes and all sorts of machinery, we have the technology to swiftly make the massive transition to various other environmentally friendly forms of energy. Electric cars are here and the technology can only get better and more efficient. Solar, wind, tidal, geothermal, and hydropower are all options. We can even create power from algae. The government must stop subsidizing oil and start subsidizing and investing in alternative energies. Jobs will be lost from the death of the oil industry, but those jobs will be replaced by the different jobs needed in a sustainable infrastructure.

13 – Stop Using Ethanol

Ethanol has been lauded by some as a means towards more energy independence, but it's not entirely clean and at best could help transition society from fossil fuels to other cleaner, more efficient energies. This is because ethanol is made from corn which in turn forces the price of corn up along with corn based foods which is most foods. With the dismal state of the economy people with lower incomes should not be forced to have to pay more for food they can already barely afford. Alternative energy technologies are here, vehicles can run on electricity, and using ethanol mostly just shifts the load-bearing weight of civilization from fossil fuels to another singular industry with its own vulnerabilities. Just like it's a bad idea to base our transportation and civilization at large on a finite resource it's also a bad idea to base them on a resource vulnerable to drought, diseases, fungi, insects, shifting agricultural regions and which also happens to be the pillar of our food supply.

14 - Invest In Infrastructure

Roads, highways, interstates, bridges, dams, power plants, railways and all manner of constructions allowing the free flow of people and goods while providing the necessary power to keep modern society thriving are the bones of our nation. Bones are literally the infrastructure of the body and the proverbial bones we call infrastructure are just as important in keeping the nation alive. Imagine a body with all of its bones broken, or breaking, and no doctors to repair them. Unfortunately that's exactly what's happening to these important structures across the nation. The maintenance for much of these constructions has been funded by a gas tax. However, the gas tax has not been raised to keep up and no wants it to be raised. Without more money, the department responsible for taking care of our nation's bones may completely run out of money and become bankrupt. Members of Congress have been looking for an alternative means of funding. But, they're still looking. Why the nation's literally failing infrastructure is not a top priority remains a mystery. Though whatever the answer to the mystery is wouldn't justify putting our nation and our people at risk. There are not enough federal inspectors to even survey all the wear and tear, let alone enough people trying to fix it.

Fixing our nations dams, roads, bridges and so on, should be of obvious importance. These things keep everything else running. While no wants more taxes, we can either pay more for gas, which would impact working people the hardest, or we can reallocate funds towards maintaining our necessary infrastructure. Another potentiality is creating a Department of Infrastructure instead of being administrated as a sub-branch of the Department of Transportation. If we do something, the worst thing that happens is nothing happens. No bridges or dams collapse and everyone goes about their day. The best thing is that we'd create jobs by putting construction companies to work and creating permanent maintenance positions. Maintaining infrastructure isn't just a good idea, it's an imperative. And if it's done, everybody wins and the chances of anyone being caught under the rubble of a collapsed bridge become much smaller.

15 - Create A Green New Deal

Climate change is here and only getting worse. The power and frequency of storms are higher than ever, wild-fire season is now year round, sea levels are rising and island communities around the world are sinking, and the list of consequences goes on for some length. Human activity is the cause; in fact human activity on the planet is so profound that geologists propose we now live in a new geological epoch called the Anthropocene. That means if humans disappeared tomorrow, evidence of our existence would still exist as a distinct layer of ground strata for millions of years. Because of human activity it's now believed we have entered the sixth mass extinction event of the planet Earth; the rate at which living things are going extinct is on par with the rates of past extinction events. These are all facets of the same problem: unsustainable and destructive human practices. And if we are to avert literal catastrophe we must create and implement a Green New Deal on a scale larger than the Marshall Plan to rebuild Europe after World War II.

First and foremost of any proposed GND must be the abolition of fossil fuels as the foundation for our infrastructure. Some strategies for ending our consumption have already been covered, but there are other, more comprehensive options too. Subsidizing electric car companies in combination with gas-car buy-back programs and tax credits for individuals would reduce the cost of electric cars thus making the transition easier for working people as gas stations are replaced with charging stations. Creating new public transit systems would also reduce the need for cars to begin with.

Power plants powering those cars today still use mostly gas and coal. We can make it so every new building must be equipped with solar panels and meet certain efficiency standards. The solar supplements will reduce demand on the grid as old power stations are decommissioned and replaced by a combination of other technologies like tidal, geothermal, wind, molten-salt reactors, and others. Constructing these new power plants and other sustainable infrastructure projects will create a period a massive employment for possibly a few decades.

We must also demand of leaders and of corporations that they act and change their means of doing business if they seek to continue doing business. Companies will no longer be allowed to destroy the planet in their unending quest for progress and profit. No more dumping into bodies of water, no more releasing toxic gases into the atmosphere, and severe restitutive and punitive punishments for transgressors.

The outcomes of these undertakings will be healthier people and thus financial savings in healthcare, saving money and lives by avoiding future disasters, an extended period of prosperity, and decreased chances of human extinction. And with an already crumbling infrastructure and lack of well-paying jobs we can use this as an opportunity to revitalize our infrastructure with new, sustainable technologies that are beneficial to the environment. We can rebuild our infrastructure better than it was; make it more efficient and sustainable all while creating new and good-paying jobs. We can begin to clean up the air, water, and land thus improving the quality of where we live and the quality of our lives.

Food and Nutrition

16 - Improve Food Safety And Nutrition

The obesity epidemic is part of a larger ongoing food crisis in America. Over one third of Americans are obese as are increasing numbers of children. The news media float different hypothesis about the cause of rising obesity rates yet seemingly always remain mystified. The root cause of obesity is our food is bad for us and the food that isn't is too expensive.

A different food is recalled every month because it's contaminated with salmonella, or E.coli, or sawdust, or whatever. Our food is also full of hard to pronounce chemical additives. Food labels should not read "100 percent organic" and "100 real food" as additional, optional selling points: food should be "100 organic" and "100 percent food" by default of being food. And of course products with those labels will cost more, and eating poorly will have larger compound costs down the line.

It's important to note that there are many different types of people and a healthy weight varies from person to person. Somebody may have a physiological condition which causes them to become obese, or an eating disorder with the same results. While individuals must take some responsibility for their actions, how much responsibility can individuals really have when they simply don't have access to quality nutrition? The majority of Americans live paycheck to paycheck, their job, or jobs, leave them with little time and leftover energy. Some people are located in "food deserts" where there are no grocery stores nearby. How can someone have personal responsibility over their weight and general health if they don't have any real control over what foods they can access and afford?

These trends need to end. All of our food should be 100 percent food. Healthier foods should cost less than chemically laden pseudo-foods. Soda should not be less expensive than water. Snacks should not be cheaper than produce. For these changes to be made there are several choices for courses of action. Buying locally grown foods can help limit our reliance on pseudo-foods. However, even farmer's markets can be more expensive because the produce is not grown and collected by machines in a streamlined process. But the more we buy from local farmers and the more we plant ourselves, the costs will eventually come down. If more people bought more at local levels it would not only drive pricing competition, but with a larger stream of steady customers local farmers could potentially make more money even with lower prices.

There's also more the government should and shouldn't be doing. Instead of giving subsidies to large agro-businesses they could instead support actual farmers. Instead of creating false scarcity the government could implement a way to disperse food based on demand and need instead of profitability. Funding and staffing for existing regulatory departments needs to be increased to an amount appropriate for inspecting facilities. The power of these agencies can be legislated into being more effective and potent instead of legislated into impotency which has been the current practice for some time.

Allowing the current system to continue is allowing companies to extort money from people by holding their nutrition hostage: pay more, or suffer the consequences of exclusively eating junk-food for years. We could all be healthier in a world with these changes. With initiatives like above, we could have declining obesity rates, declining obesity related illnesses, and declining healthcare costs. We should all be able to eat well and eat affordably.

17 - Fortify National Food Security

While Big Agro-Businesses continue to take advantage of farmers and consumers, the means by which they produce our food put's us all in further jeopardy and harm the environment in numerous ways. Traces of toxic chemicals used to deter pests and weeds are found on produce. Chemical pesticides and fertilizers flow into rivers and bays creating aquatic dead zones. Insects exposed to pesticides also poison larger animals when they eaten. Furthermore, these chemicals only kill *most* of the insects and pests allowing them to grow immune over time thus rendering the pesticides obsolete and leaving our food vulnerable to new, hardier variants of familiar pests. Many agro-businesses also practice mono-cropping which is a way of planting crops in which individual plants are all genetically identical leaving them all vulnerable to any particularly virulent disease, or fungi.

Potentially we could force these businesses to change their methods through legislation, boycotts, or combination of these and other tactics like supporting local famers. Technologies and agricultural methods exist to grow food with less space, less water and resource consumption and are environmentally sustainable. These businesses have a choice: either diversify by dismantling their toxic and archaic methods which increase our risks of consuming toxins and of large scale famine in favor of numerous small farms which have a genetic diversity within their crops and utilize natural pest deterrents, or be run out of business altogether by the people.

18 - Abolish Factory Farms

Perhaps worse than agro-businesses are factory farms which are where the bulk of our poultry and meat products come from. These factories keep animals like chickens, pigs, turkeys, and cows in spaces so small they cannot even turn around. They are crammed together by the hundreds and thousands. These factories are horrific abusers of animals: clipping off beaks of chickens because they'll get agitated and peck at each other from being so close together. Male chicks are ground up alive. The female chickens often spend their entire lives in darkness.

Chickens and turkeys are fed so much and given hormones so they grow larger and faster than they would naturally, so much so they often become incapacitated by their own weight. Cattle might live outdoors, but are also confined to overcrowded plots of land which extend for acres. These animals are also given antibiotics and hormones while they "walk" about nearly up to their knees in mud and their own waste. These cattle live covered in their own filth and when they're butchered it's impossible to not get some of their waste mixed in with the meat. Factory farms are also extremely bad for the environment and, along with other unsustainable agricultural methods, contribute possibly the most to climate change. They contaminate local water sources and often leave nearby towns permanently shrouded in a foul stench which often leads to medical issues for the residents of these towns.

While these practices help keep prices low, they cost employees, animals, and environment a great deal. Smaller, more localized ranches and farms may not be as efficient but they are healthier for the people, the animals, and the environment. The overuse of antibiotics in animals can also lead to antibiotic resistant strains of bacteria which can spread rapidly between animals in such confined spaces. This practice increases the risk of some pathogen infecting large populations of animals which puts our national food security at risk and increases the chances of some pathogen jumping from animals to humans. These unhealthy practices go unregulated and unchecked. Even the laws and guidelines in place are easily ignored and go unenforced. We must demand better oversight and eventually abolish these practices altogether through legislation and boycotts. Instead of subsidizing these institutions our money would be better spent investing in local sustainable farms and ranches.

19 - Destroy "Big Food" Monopolies

"Big Agro," and "Big Food" have also been gaining an undeserved and unhealthy influence with Congress to enact legislation that benefits and protects corporate interests over individuals and society. There are also now food monopolies that exist and crush potential market competition and limit consumer options.

Private interests are responsible for deregulation and defunding regulatory enforcement agencies which have exacerbated many existing problems. Food safety is in a poor state to say the least as are the working conditions for people in these factory farms and Big Agro fields. Employees are exploited and abused: working for low pay while being exposed to toxic chemicals and biologically hazardous materials; fired for calling out because of injuries sustained on the job; threatened with termination if they report their injuries; and sometimes withholding pay for some reason or another.

Big Agro businesses are also responsible for putting smaller farms out of business and not just because they can undercut most any small farmer's prices. Lots of small, local farms are contracted to help serve in some capacity like breeding the animals, but are then contractually obligated to pay the company for unnecessary upgrades that the company itself continuously comes up with. Kept in perpetual debt and unable fulfill their contractual obligations the farmers are then forced to forfeit their land – which was the plan the whole time.

Business practices like this cannot be tolerated and must be abolished and may already be illegal under current anti-trust laws. We must demand these laws be enforced and others implemented to cease these practices. We must vote for candidates without ties to Big Agro and demand others in Congress to sever any and all ties they might have. This is why we have representatives, they are meant to represent us, the people, their constituents and not corporate profits.

20 - Make All School Lunches Free

While many schools offer free or reduced lunches some families do not meet the requirements and the costs are still burdensome. Some schools have banned peanut butter because some students have peanut allergies and some have banned school lunches altogether, believing that school lunches are healthier than what students would bring in from home, thus forcing families to pay for school lunches. Students have been shamed and made to go hungry because they couldn't afford to eat. That's no way to treat a child and is a terrible way to encourage active learning in a school environment.

Schools shouldn't be banning peanut butter or home lunches unless they begin paying for them. Prisoners are served three free meals everyday thanks to taxpayers, certainly the same courtesy can be afforded to school children. Every student should be eligible for free school food and the food should not only be healthy, but quality enough so the students can actually enjoy eating it. To force a child to go hungry because their parents aren't wealthy enough, or maybe just because they forget their lunch money at home, is inhuman. But making school lunches free for children isn't enough.

21 - Create Universal Nutrition Accessibility

Starvation exists in United States right now and at the same time obesity and related illnesses are at record highs. Most Americans live paycheck to paycheck and make less than $30,000 a year and the simple fact is not everyone can afford to eat and those who can are forced to purchase cheap pseudo-foods with little nutritional benefit. This is systemic classism at best and premeditated class warfare at worst. This system contributes to keeping the poor disenfranchised: as prices go up people need to work more and can buy less; nutrition deficient diets contribute to all sorts of health problems which cost money to treat thus compounding the cycles of poverty further. Many people also live in "food deserts" where it's more difficult to even get to a grocery store.

Instead of government subsidies going to multimillion dollar food industries, subsidies could be reallocated to local farmers and ranchers making food cheaper to buy and more profitable to grow. Local food initiatives could also be started, like community garden projects. Food and quality nutrition need to also be recognized as human rights. All other animal species on the planet can simply go out and find food if they're hungry.

Humans are dependent on a system of economics rigged by wealthy elites. Nutrition is a biological need and a natural right and it's time it be treated as such.

Medical

22 - Enact Universal Healthcare

Every day people are suffering and dying in the United States because they can't afford medical treatment; they can't afford their prescriptions, or epi-pens let alone surgery if need be. Tens of thousands die every year and millions more are left devastated by debt. People dying simply because they're poor is unacceptable and should be unthinkable for the nation that went to the moon, the world's remaining super-power.

Healthcare should be treated as a human right and should be available for everyone especially in one of the world's most productive, wealthy, and developed nations. Giving people healthcare, taking care of our fellows is just human decency and should be as comprehensive as possible. That would be an achievement we can show the world and lead by example, something to have national pride in. If that's not enough, the pragmatism of comprehensive healthcare for all should be obvious: healthier citizens will be happier citizens; people who get sick less miss work less which is good for employers and employees; providing preventive healthcare keeps emergency room visits and disease rates down, which will help to decrease the overall costs of healthcare.

There are ways to provide access to quality healthcare for everyone in the US including the homeless. For instance we could raise taxes on the wealthiest Americans, or reallocate money from our bloated defense budget. The Affordable Care Act, colloquially called "Obamacare" was a step in the right direction, but it's not enough. We need to cover everyone with something like Medicare for all which will save money and save lives.

23 - Create Mental Health Infrastructure

Undiagnosed and, or untreated mental illnesses are wreaking havoc on people's lives across the country every day. Stigmas keep some people from seeking professional help while some can't afford another expense, or both. Regardless, ignoring a mental illness is like ignoring an infection: it's going to get worse.

We know mental illnesses are in fact physical illnesses. The physical natures of mental disorders are located in the brain and can be created by physical trauma, physical abnormalities, neurochemical imbalances, or some combination thereof. Certainly these ailments can also be caused by traumatic events, environmental factors, or be inherited genetically and they can no more be willed away than cancer, or a bullet wound. Despite our understanding and our immense wealth as a nation a very large portion of the homeless are mentally ill simply because they have nowhere else to go and their illnesses go untreated. And a sizeable percentage of those are veterans suffering from ailments like post-traumatic stress disorder, or PTSD.

Ostracizing people for reasons beyond their control and simply letting them fall through the cracks is appalling. We have the resources to lessen their suffering and to get people the help they need. While some individuals may be unable to live independently and require some facility, or assistance, they shouldn't be left on the streets struggling to survive. But by and large most people suffering from mental illnesses can become productive members of society if they receive a little help. Would it not be better to lessen human suffering, decrease the number of people without homes, and add people to contribute to the economy as opposed to letting people suffer and die on the streets just because they're sick?

Homelessness is just one extreme case of the potential consequences of untreated mental illness, but other extremes like suicide or substance abuse are potentialities too. Smaller consequences also stack up over time as a mental illness deteriorates a person's physical health and well-being. We need to create a mental health infrastructure beginning in schools with a combination of education and services. We can extend those services up through adulthood by making mental health professionals as accessible as a primary care physician. We must all be more understanding of what these illnesses actually are because stigmas against mental illness and their treatments like therapy hold all of us back.

24 - Stop Diagnosing Natural Childhood Behaviors As Disorders

Children who do not behave like little adults are medicated into docility. Attention Deficit and Hyperactivity Disorder, or ADHD diagnoses along with diagnoses of other behavioral disorders have increased dramatically over the last two decades. Part of this may be from better diagnostic techniques, or just a general rise in awareness about these conditions like what's happened with autism. While these are real disorders, many of the people diagnosed are children who have trouble focusing and sitting still during school. The problem is that's just what kids do. Children usually have a lot of energy and short attention spans. Expecting them to sit still and be quiet for 6-8 hours a day for school is just obtuse. Those tasks are difficult for most adults to do. And when students don't behave exactly as they're expected to they're diagnosed and given powerful drugs, many with terrible side-effects. Children who do become medicated are often described even by their parents as becoming "zombiefied."

Some people genuinely benefit from medication, but first, alternatives to medications like therapy and letting kids have more outside time need to be tried. Second, school shouldn't be as long as it is. As mentioned earlier, there are different ways that people learn, and the children that don't learn well from lectures may need something more hands on and more engaging. Third, we may just need to change our expectations for our children: expect them to loud, expect them to get bored sitting at a desk all day, expect them to misbehave and get into some trouble because that's what kids do. Before children are medicated these other possibilities should be seriously explored. Parents are obviously the primary people responsible for exploring these other possibilities, but society and our institutions of education have a responsibility to make school more conducive to learning for all different learning types. Instead of forcing people to fit a mold we should create a mold that fits people. The benefits should be clear. These changes would create happier students, more productive students, less medicated children and ultimately happier, healthier adults.

25 - Implement Stronger Vaccination Policies

Diseases thought eradicated by vaccines are back thanks entirely to the Anti-Vax movement. There are no credible studies supporting any of the claims by the anti-vaccine community ranging from vaccines efficacy to the claim that vaccines cause autism. Anti-vaccine supporters falsely link the increase in autism diagnoses and the increase in the number of vaccines as proof that vaccines are the cause of autism, but, correlation does not equal causation. The most likely scenario is simply an increase in awareness and diagnostic tools to detect autism thus accounting for the spike. And if that's not the reason for the spike there are numerous other possible causes which may be linked to the environment and toxins found therein, but not vaccines. Even if vaccines did cause autism, they still keep children alive and safe from contracting deadly diseases.

To counter this issue, vaccines could be mandated by law, but controlling what people put into their bodies isn't something we should pursue. But vaccination in not solely an issue of individual liberty: it's about the children of parents who opt out of vaccinations and all the people those children come into contact with, some of whom haven't been vaccinated yet, or are immunocompromised. These people who have no choice are at risk. So, while it is a public health issue and while the government still shouldn't be able to dictate what people put, or don't put, in their bodies we already have compromises that can be expanded. For instance, most schools already have some sort of mandatory vaccine policy. More schools could adopt such an approach and let children who don't get vaccinated either be home schooled or attend a like-minded private school.

We as a society must also become more accurately informed and weigh the risks: even if vaccines did cause autism, the possibility of autism is much better than bringing back an epidemic of preventable diseases and dead children. Furthermore, any cases where an unvaccinated child develops a preventable disease and dies, or causes a larger outbreak among vulnerable populations the parents responsible should be tried for criminal negligence, or manslaughter.

26 - Allow Universal Access To Contraception

A medicine exists that could benefit nearly fifty percent of the population, but access to it and other related treatments are increasingly prohibitive because of religious ideologies and sexism. Birth control options like "the pill," help prevent unwanted pregnancies and therefore abortions too, but also help treat certain medical conditions. Loopholes still exist that allow insurers to not cover contraception despite its benefits for women's health. Numerous state legislatures also try to undermine the choices and health of women by passing bills restricting access to contraceptive options.

We must demand fundamental women's health options be covered by insurers and close the loopholes in current legislation. More than that, legislation needs to be passed protecting women's health from further subversion. We also need to vote out legislators who actively pursue policies that are harmful to women.

27 - Protect Women's Bodily Autonomy

Despite Roe vs. Wade allowing for legal abortions women's bodies are more heavily regulated than guns. The utilization of birth control is controversial and for many women accessing it remains problematic. Centers that perform abortions are legally allowed to exist, but some legislators are undermining their existence by requiring facilities follow unnecessary and nonsensical building codes. In some states it's already difficult to find a facility that can perform abortions even when medical complications place the mother's health in jeopardy. And furthermore, certain medical procedures for women even require spousal consent.

The law must recognize we all have the right to bodily autonomy and it may not discriminate on the basis of sex. We must protect the rights recognized by the Roe vs. Wade decision by placing the same and more encompassing protections within state constitutions.

28 - Destroy "Big Pharma"

Pharmaceutical companies are companies first and foremost and profit comes first. They market new drugs directly to the public which is a problem in and of itself; marketing drugs to the general public often creates the perception of necessity when there isn't any. Then those same drugs need to be recalled a few years later. Pharmaceutical industries also market their new drugs directly to doctors which is at least in part for the opioid crises. Doctors are given money or gifts in exchange for prescribing certain brands, or specific medications. This incentivizes health professionals to choose certain medications over others even if it's not in a patient's best interests and encourages them to overprescribe medications like addictive pain killers. At the same time many lobby Congress to keep safe and natural alternatives like cannabis criminalized, while others lobby Congress in the other direction because they're poised to enter and monopolize the market.

Big Pharma companies also spend a great deal more money on marketing and the salaries of CEOs than they do on actual research and development. They also price gouge lifesaving treatments that cost pennies to make. It also begs the question that if a cure for certain diseases like cancer were to be discovered would they reveal it? If they cure a disease, their customers will stop coming back. Or if they reveal it, would they then charge immense amounts of money for it?

Pharmaceutical companies need to change how they do business at a fundamental level of be legislated out of existence. We may be better off without drug companies at all and instead replacing them with non-profit research centers. What they, or their replacements must focus on are people over profits; holistic approaches limiting the number of side effects over rushing new products to market; innovation over inordinate salaries. Both companies and doctors should not be manipulating their way into more money by improperly and over prescribing medications, but since they have been both need to be investigated for their respective roles in the ongoing opioid crisis that's destroying lives and families every day. Appropriate civil and criminal charges should then be filed and pursued vigorously. The same should be done to those who price gouge and extort money from customers in exchange for the lifesaving treatments they need. In addition to civil and criminal charges, considering the scope of devastation and the disgusting nature of this particularly callous strain of greed, punitive damages need to be brought against all responsible.

Civil Rights

29 - Make Election Day A National Holiday

Holding elections on Tuesdays and not having it be a national holiday so people can take the day off from work to vote is a means to disenfranchise working voters. Politicians have ways of disenfranchising voters who would vote against them ranging from gerrymandering to voter ID laws and holding elections on a workday is no exception.

Some argue that the polls are open long enough for everyone to make it. That's just not true, particularly for people who must work more than one job. They are then forced between making the money they need and voting. Others may have the time to get to the polls, but their polling places are understaffed and overcrowded creating long and unpredictable wait times.

Increasing the difficulty for working people to vote is a violation of their Civil Rights. Elections can't just be moved to weekends because plenty of people work on weekends. The solution is straightforward though: all election days must be made into paid holidays so anyone and everyone who would like to vote may do so easily and without financial restriction of lost time and pay. This would likely drive the number actual voters up considerably giving us more accurate representation and a more engaged citizenry.

30 - Rein In Eminent Domain

The government grossly abuses eminent domain laws to benefit corporations by seizing land from homeowners and giving it to private business interests. Sometimes eminent domain is necessary for building roads, dams, perhaps schools, or hospitals, or other public goods and services and those instances should be rare. Unfortunately it's used more often now for the creation of things like mall developments and oil pipelines. Pipelines for example have nothing to do with the public good, but people are still displaced from their homes so some oil companies can make more profit while poisoning water and the land whenever their lines leak – which is regularly. Abuses like this should never be tolerated. We have a right to property and if a business wants our land then they must convince the owners to sell, end of process. It's absurd to remove people from their homes, some of whom have lived in an area for generations, for almost any reason, let alone to make way for corporate profits which, particularly in the case of pipelines, are detrimental to the public good.

We must urge or state and federal leaders to revise these laws in favor of land owners particularly in these economic times where many are lucky to have an apartment, let alone a home and land. We must enact new laws and enforce old ones that explicitly forbid the use of eminent domain for the benefit of corporations. Furthermore, any member of government found to have abused these laws and powers should at best be forced to resign, and at worst punitively punished to the full extent of the law. In cases like these it should also be well within the rights of private citizens to defend their land with force if need be. Large businesses have enough power and influence and it's time we the people have more ways to combat the powers that be and to secure our rights.

31 - Protect Marriage Equality

Although marriage equality is a civil right and currently the law of the land, we have a very different Supreme Court and challenges are already being made. Objections are usually religious in nature and while marriage is historically a religious ceremony it's also an institution of the law. Marriage comes with legal aspects like tax benefits, hospital visitation rights, alongside other considerations and it's unconstitutional to deny anyone these rights based on religion, race, or sexual orientation. We have the freedom of religion, but also provisions which limit the actions of religious people in the Constitution. This means people can believe and do what they like so long as it does not interfere with the rights of anyone else. Regardless of a person's personal beliefs concerning homosexuality, just like gender and race, they must be treated equally under the law.

It is up to us to demand and pressure state legislatures to pass bills reinforcing the protections of marriage equality. At the same time we should lobby Congress for an amendment to the Constitution clearly defining and protecting marriage equality. We must of course be ready to fight back should a new case come before the Supreme Court and the new "Justices" deliver a draconian decision.

32 - End Sexist And Racist Pay Gaps

Black people, women, LGBTQ individuals, and other minorities are paid less compared to their straight, white, male counterparts. These populations are also more likely to suffer from sexual assault, domestic violence, police brutality and other forms of discrimination. The pay gaps are a systemic means to disenfranchise certain populations. They make life financially more difficult: they make it more difficult for people to leave bad situations, pursue legal action if need be, recover from unforeseeable expenses, and to actively participate in our democracy.

We must demand our legislators enact more protections for these individuals that will make it easier to bring lawsuits against companies for discriminatory pay and discrimination in hiring processes. We also need to move towards pay transparency: the saying "never talk about your salary" is only meant to keep workers in the dark and take away the advantage when negotiating raises and salaries .This requires us to vote in legislators that will do what needs to be done and pressure the ones already there.

Ending the pay gap is far more than just a symbolic gesture of equality. If we can end the pay gaps we can also give more people resources to better fight injustices themselves. Financial stability makes it easier to escape an abusive relationship, makes it easier to pursue legal recourse in other instances of discrimination, and makes it easier just to rebound from unexpected costs.

33 - End The "Pink Tax"

Women are paid less than men and often have to pay more for the same things. Some will argue this gender price gap is the result of women's products costing more to produce, but the prices suggest that there should be something more than the mere change in color. It's not just that prices are higher, but they're also higher more often. This is sometimes called the "Pink Tax." This is sometimes called the "Pink Tax." The costs may seem small, but they add up to hundreds, if not thousands of dollars annually for an individual woman. For low-income women and single mothers it might mean having to choose between grocery shopping and paying rent; between car insurance and heating the house. Price gaps are the economic symptoms of a culture that devalues and alienates women by paying them less and charging them more for the same things as men, respectively.

We need to officially address this unofficial taxation. Potentially things like feminine hygiene products, diapers, toilet paper, and similar items should have any taxes removed. This would help alleviate some of the financial burden of both women and parents. We can enact certain legislation to create and enforce penalties for people and corporations that artificially inflate prices on products marketed towards women.

34 - Ban Gay Conversion Therapy

Gay conversation therapy, also known as reparative therapy, uses widely debunked pseudoscience to justify inflicting enough emotional trauma to trigger involuntary responses normal human emotions, thoughts, and behaviors. It's not dissimilar in principle to how the Ludovico technique works in "A Clockwork Orange."

The notion that homosexuals are homosexuals by choice, or that it is in anyway something to be cured, is an absurdity without foundation. This form of "therapy" can cause anxiety, depression, and an increased likelihood of both abusing drugs and suicide attempts. Furthermore, it legitimizes bigotry based on religious and pseudoscientific grounds against people for something that's normal, intrinsic, natural, and healthy - just like the attribute of skin color. Some states have already passed legislated that no licensed medical professional can recommend conversion therapy, nor are insurance companies allowed to pay for such therapy. Similar, and perhaps further reaching laws, should be adopted either by the states, or federally, to disallow reparative therapists from pretending to be legitimate health professionals, just as palm readers as disallowed from pretending to be stockbrokers. Furthermore, the individuals who have practiced this technique should be tried for assault and torture.

35 – Recognize LGBTQ Rights As Human Rights

The LGBTQ community while much more accepted today we still have a long ways to go before reaching equality. For instance, people with non-binary gender identities are discriminated against in life threatening ways every day. Transgender people are, and have been, a targeted population: despite their relatively small percentage of the population they experience disproportionately high rates of homelessness, abuse, suicide attempts, police brutality, and other forms of discrimination like the previously mentioned pay gap. Contemporary "bathroom bills" and similar acts serve only to further harass and alienate this population while feeding into fear mongering ignorance.

Instead of actively campaigning against Trans people, states and legislators should be actively campaigning for the equal treatment and protection of trans individuals. Through these campaigns and perhaps with comprehensive education programs in schools, the general population can better learn who these people are and that there's no reason to fear, or mistreat, them. Discriminating against someone because of their sexual identity is the same as any other form of discrimination. It must therefore be declared that in legislation, if not a constitutional amendment that Trans rights are human rights.

36 - Fight Obesity Discrimination

Overweight people are also the targets of derision and discrimination. Some employers will not hire obese people and in some cases, particularly concerning waitresses, will fire them for gaining weight. Obesity is a rising health concern in US and is not always a simple case of personal responsibility, or lack thereof.

Unless an individual can literally not do the job they cannot be refused a position because of their weight and body shape. If a person's obesity is the result of a medical condition or some other reason beyond their control and cannot work because of it they should qualify for disability. Recent discrimination cases have turned obesity into a Civil Rights issue. And now we must and fight it, again with legislation, education and the aforementioned reforms to food production and quality.

37 - End Violence Against Protestors

Pepper sprayed, tear gassed, beaten, shot with rubber bullets and firehoses, attacked by dogs: these are the realities for unarmed, peaceful protesters and activists.

Police exacerbate confrontational situations and their tactics are often responsible for instigating riots from protests. These are examples of oppression meant to destroy dissent which are clearly violations of our Constitution and in some cases basic human rights. Yet interestingly, for some reason, when religious zealots picket funerals of dead soldiers, white supremacists march down Main Street carrying torches, and fascist gangs do everything they can to make demonstrations turn violent the police suddenly become pacifists.

Attacking protestors is one of the hallmarks of authoritarianism and cannot be allowed to continue if we wish to call ourselves a democracy, or "the land of the free." Protest is a form of expression and assembly, both of which are explicitly protected by the First Amendment of The Bill of Rights; it is our means of being heard when the system fails and our leaders refuse to listen. Using violence against activists is unnecessary and counterproductive, usually just inspiring further demonstrations. Instead, the underlying problems must be dealt with or nothing will change. Civil unrest will remain, continuing to build until riots become the default form of political engagement. We must demand our leaders hear us and demand the protections for these First Amendment rights be enforced.

38 - Stop Arresting Protestors

Our civil liberties are being violated by non-violent means as well. After protestors have been beaten up and bloodied they're arrested and charged with "unlawful assembly" or whatever else anti-protest legislation allows them to get away with. In many states legislatures have taken it upon themselves to regulate the right to protest into impotency: time restrictions, the implementation of "free speech zones" which are often located away from the public eye often consisting of a chain link kennel. Journalists reporting on demonstrations have also been arrested as protestors themselves.

First, we must vote for individuals who will listen to us. But, when our rights are violated we must also hold those who violate them accountable. We must demand the resignations of all legislators who have crafted and supported legislation making it more difficult to hold demonstrations while making it easier to be arrested at them. We must demand that the laws protecting our rights be enforced, not subverted and if they still refuse to listen we will enforce them ourselves.

39 - End Mass Surveillance

We live under constant surveillance. It's not paranoid or unrealistic even, to suspect someone might be watching you. Governmental agencies like the NSA and CIA spy on every single American daily. They collect and store our data; they can turn the cameras and microphones of any phone or computer on remotely; even local police departments seize our personal data without a warrant through the use of new technologies. Security and traffic cameras are at their disposal too, which combined with our other data enables computer programs to build predictive behavioral models of individuals and populations. This massive, unprecedented surveillance state is responsible for false arrests and utilized as a tool to disrupt protests and harass organizers. These programs invade our privacy; cost absurd amounts of money, time, and resources that could be better allocated and more efficiently used; lead to false imprisonment; are abused for political reasons; have never stopped a terrorist attack; and the potential for further abuse is a certainty if we do nothing.

Since these actions are equatable to unlawful searches and seizures of private information individuals can file lawsuits against the perpetrators. Any law allowing this to happen should be challenged in the courts. Current laws, like those in the Bill of Rights for example, need to be enforced so our rights are protected and new ones instituted expressly forbidding these actions. The web and its services, for better or worse, are integral to our modern lives, so much so that they've become difficult to escape and should be recognized as a public utility. Current mass surveillance and US history make it clear we should defund, or completely abolish agencies like the CIA and NSA.

40 - Repeal The Patriot Act

Indefinite detention is a scenario American citizens within the US have found themselves in. Laws like the Patriot Act and the National Defense Authorization Act, or NDAA undermines the Constitution, specifically the Bill of Rights by making it legal to discard due process and our other rights if we're suspected of terrorism. Laws like the Patriot Act grant far reaching powers and were intentionally written with vague language to leave them open to the broadest possible interpretations. Poorly defined wording makes it possible to consider almost anyone a potential terrorist threat. Laws disbanding our civil liberties also set precedents which enable the surveillance state uses as justification to expand.

We are not safer because of these acts. Arguably they don't even make people feel safer, but instead make them fearful that they'll become a suspected terrorists due to some misidentification, faulty information, or political differences. Anyone can be detained and the only thing needed to justify their detainment is something, anything, linking them in some way to terrorism which is easy since "terrorism" is open to interpretation. The laws' potential for abuse seems to be a potential the government is actively trying to fulfil. Removing juries, due process, and other legal rights is both frighteningly totalitarian and blatantly unconstitutional. Even terrorists deserve a trial because when we start stripping rights away from one person it's usually the start of taking them away from everyone. Suspects are legally considered innocent until proven guilty and no one wants to put an innocent person behind bars or potentially sentenced to death.

We cannot allow laws like this to stand. We must demand they be repealed through petitioning our representatives, protests, legal action when possible, and most importantly voting for representatives that will not endorse a similar bill and who's willing to fight to repeal the current laws that strip away our rights. These laws were reactionary and passed out of the fear following the 9/11 attacks and when we bend to fear, when we bend to terror, when we exchange liberty for security and allow terrorists to shape our laws we give them a victory.

41 - Eliminate "Black Sites"

Ironically it's no secret that the US operates numerous secret prisons, or "black sites." These sites exist around the globe and are exempt from Constitutional law. Black sites are intended to be places where suspected terrorists and national security threats are held without trial. These sites are a stain on our nation's reputation and moral authority. Innocent people have been tortured and killed in places like Guantanamo Bay and other military prisons. Additionally, the operation of these places and detaining of people without trials, evidence, or warrants gives our enemies more reason and justification for attacking us.

Violations of Constitutional and human rights should never be infringed. We cannot allow our government and its agencies to act outside the law, nor can we allow them to continue to claim transparency when they operate secret prisons and black sites which are literally the opposite of transparency. It's far more likely these places and the practices inside them endanger us all by inspiring detained individuals, or their families to seek retribution.

42 - Justice For The Tortured

The US Government is responsible for using torture on detainees without so much as a trial, or even evidence. The horrible treatment of detainees was excused in the name of national security, but no significant information was gained and, even worse, innocent people were detained and tortured. People died as a result and instead of effectively combating terrorism it just gave people more reason to hate the United States. Instead of immediately owning up to these misdeeds, it took years of scandal, investigation, and debating what exactly constitutes torture. Instead of remaining true to American values and championing human rights, top officials cowered and used fear to justify torture, betraying the Constitution and their humanity in the process.

Cruel and unusual punishment is expressly forbidden by our Constitution and we cannot fight extremism creating oppressed and justifiably angry populations. Nor can we claim to be the "land of the free" with "liberty and justice for all" while participating in torture behind closed doors. Torture cannot be condoned and we must demand justice for those who have suffered unjustly. Those who allowed these actions to take place and those who ordered them must be held accountable and brought to trial. The government must also pay restitution to survivors and families of the deceased. While these actions cannot be undone, we can universally condemn them and those involved and do everything we can to ensure it never happens again.

Law Enforcement

43 - Repeal Restrictive "Off-Grid" Laws

Across the country the states have found ways to penalize people for self-sufficiency and living off-grid. Most places don't have laws that address off-grid living specifically, but instead certain aspects of off-grid living are said to violate existing ordinances: restricting how long someone can "camp" on their own property even while a proper house is being built; requiring a stable connection to electricity, but not counting solar panels, or wind turbines; mandating occupants have access to clean water, but not counting wells and water cisterns; along with other over restrictive regulations. The situation is made more ridiculous by the fact that while wells and cisterns are be considered unsafe, but it's public water grids in places like Flint, Michigan and other cities across the country that are contaminated with lead and other chemicals. Together, laws like these are called off-grid laws and serve as mechanisms of control: they force people to pay utility companies for services the property owners don't want or need; and when people refuse they're fined and if they still refuse they're jailed. We're experiencing a housing crisis already and these laws compound that problem by creating an undue economic burden on people.

Restrictive ordinances need to be loosened and some entirely repealed. They must also be challenged in court. And instead of making it more difficult for Americans to become self-sufficient we should be making it easier. We could fully subsidize solar panels for all homeowners so they can create the decentralized grid of the future where electricity comes from every building and excess energy is transferred into the grid and distributed as needed. We could do similar things with wind turbines and water cisterns essentially having individuals upgrade parts of our infrastructure one at a time.

44 - Legalize Prostitution

Human beings have and enjoy sex. For consenting adults it's legal to have sex, it's legal to sell services, it's legal to be paid to have sex if it's being filmed, so why not make it legal to sell sexual services? The only arguments against treating it like any other business are religious, or puritanical in nature. Sex is not some sinful act to only be spoken of in whispers, or never at all; it's a normal and healthy human behavior. Prostitution is also made more dangerous for sex workers when the practice is prohibited because there's no support structure to keep sex workers safe from dangerous people; there are no mandatory STD screenings; and they can't go to the police to report a crime without risking their own freedom. Furthermore, keeping prostitution illegal does nothing to stop the demand which is commonly met by sex slaves controlled by pimps.

Legalizing prostitution would make the profession safer for the sex workers themselves. Treating it like any other business would limit the number of sexually transmitted infections because of mandatory medical screening and would also allow sex workers to conduct business from the safety of a fixed location. Sex workers could also go to the police if need be without the fear of being imprisoned themselves. The creation of legal brothels would also likely decrease the black market demand supplied by human trafficking.

45 - Legalize Cannabis

Cannabis is proven to be less dangerous than alcohol, cigarettes, or prescription drugs while having medical benefits of its own, yet in many states and at the federal level the drug is still prohibited. More states are decriminalizing its use, allowing medicinal use, and some even permit recreation use. The states that have allowed its legalization have seen millions of dollars in tax revenue from business and a reduction in costs from penalizing those in possession of the drug. Cannabis is still illegal in many states and under federal law it's scheduled as one of the most dangerous drugs despite all the evidence to the contrary.

Instead of arresting people on marijuana related charges, which costs taxpayers to keep them in prison, cannabis should be legalized and regulated. We already know prohibition doesn't work and people will find a way to acquire the drug. Keeping it illegal makes criminals out of regular people and keeps actual criminals in business. Legalization would result in jobs and new businesses: cultivators, store owners and employees, and manufacturing jobs for turning the rest of the plant in usable including paper, rope, clothing, and even building material in the form of hemp products. Ending cannabis prohibition would also make the drug safer since dealers occasionally mix it with other drugs, but this would no longer be the case if it can be purchased from legitimate businesses and local growers. The plant can be taxed and so can the businesses selling it thus increasing a state's revenue. And places that have enacted legalization have shown little or no spike in cannabis usage.

Most importantly, the criminalization of cannabis use and the War on Drugs are tools used to disproportionately incarcerate the poor and especially minorities. The archaic prohibition of a harmless plant, not use of the plant itself, is responsible for costing millions of people their freedom and some their lives. Cannabis legalization is therefore a necessity for justice and for dismantling institutional racism. When legalization takes place everyone imprisoned for its possession and sale must be released from and compensated for their unjust prison sentence.

46 - Decriminalize All Drug Use

1 in every 100 Americans is part of the penal system: either in prison, on probation, or on parole. So many inmates are doing extended time behind bars for non-violent, often victimless crimes and are usually placed with other, more violent offenders. Little to no effort is put towards rehabilitating and reforming these people. Instead, drug offenders come out worse than they were before and can no longer find a job with a criminal record. Many drugs pose a serious health risk to the users, but that simply means it's a medical issue for health professionals and not armed law enforcement agents. Despite common perceptions among lay-folk, scientists, doctors, and trained health professionals are certain that addiction is a legitimate disease with physical restructuring of neural pathways. The War on Drugs is a war on sick people that costs billions of dollars and countless lives every year.

For the sake of reason and compassion we have a moral obligation to bring the War on Drugs to an end by decriminalizing all drugs regardless of their nature. Decriminalization is already a successful public policy in Portugal and a handful of other countries. The best way to combat drug use is not by turning people into criminals for simply using a substance on themselves of their own volition. We combat drug problems by combating pain, sickness, and the underlying causes of addiction with medical treatment and understanding. At the very least decriminalization will reduce the number of people in prison and the number of people with difficulty finding work because of a drug related conviction. Fewer people in prison will save taxpayers money and will also make space to keep actual criminals locked up instead of letting them out early to make way for newly convicted drug offenders. Furthermore, anyone doing extended time for possession should be released from prison, compensated for their unjust imprisonment, and given access to resources to overcome their addiction.

47 - End Police Quotas

Despite being illegal in most places, police are still ordered to meet certain "quotas." Unofficial quotas are instituted by performance standards whereby officers are told they may look lazy or incompetent if they don't hand out enough tickets, or make so many arrests. Essentially police officers are creating offenders out of the general public further betraying what little trust people have left in police officers. Issuing fines for all sorts of non-crimes, like jaywalking and loitering, target the poor and minorities often forcing additional financial hardship upon already struggling families. And we can only guess how many of the fatal escalations by police officers were only initiated because they were trying to meet a quota.

This is bad law enforcement, direct contradiction to the "protect and serve" model, and illegal. We must demand civilian oversight of police departments. The police cannot be trusted in general and can no longer be permitted to regulate and investigate themselves. Departments shall be mandated to keep meticulous records and make them available online to the public. There must also be stronger consequences for those who mandate, or coerce, quotas from their officers.

48 - Stop Literal Over-Policing

We have the world's largest prison population both as a percentage of our population incarcerated and in the total number of prisoners. This is largely due to the War on Drugs. However, more and more actions are becoming illegal and punishable by incarceration. Cases of over-policing are many and varied. School children misbehaving have been taken out of class in handcuffs for matters that used to be handled by an after school detention, or even a stern reprimand from a teacher. There are instances of parents being arrested for letting their children play outside. Commuters waiting for a bus can be considered loitering and subsequently arrested. The number of sex offenders has skyrocketed, largely because the definition is being broadly applied to children playing doctor to public urination.

Over-policing is a very real, dangerous, and Orwellian phenomenon.

Over-policing cannot continue; it hurts the economy by increasing prison and court costs, and by increasing the number of people who will be unemployable because of a criminal record. The human cost is even worse. It forces people into prison, effectively ruing the rest of their lives. And all because of some trivial or entirely fabricated transgression like driving without a seatbelt? The law isn't meant to be applied so harshly to so many, that is not the spirit of, or reason we have laws at all. The spirit of law is to maintain peace and order, not to oppress populations by arresting and jailing them for any perceived misdeed. We must fight it in the courts as best we can and protest unjust arrests. Slashing funding for police departments found acting against the public is also a potential option.

49 - Stop Policing For Profit

When the Department of Justice released its report on Ferguson it revealed that most of the city's revenue was generated by issuing as many tickets and citations as the police could dream up. Police acting as agents of revenue generation isn't confined to Ferguson, Missouri, it's a problem around the country and now private companies have stepped in to handle all the fines and fees. Private companies then exacerbate the problem especially among the poor who cannot afford to pay these right away. While some may offer a payment plan, the money that people pay goes towards overdue fees first rather than the actual fine which leaves the fine in place to collect more overdue fees. What may have been a small fine can end up costing hundreds of dollars. Counties and companies are now using small traffic and other petty violations to create revenue and it disproportionally hurts the poor. Policing for profit is extortion and profit is not the objective of law enforcement.

Laws should be implemented banning private companies from being injected into the legal system like along with making it illegal for police departments to issue excessive and unnecessary citations. Counties cannot continue generating their revenue by fining their citizens into poverty. We must create civilian groups that revue all police records including financial records. If they're found to be abusing their powers to extort citizens then the police departments and county officials must be forced to resign, compensate their victims, pay punitive damages, and possibly face jail time. The police need to be policed themselves.

50 - Cease The Reemergence Of Debtor Prisons

Despite being illegal people are being sent to jail because they can't pay their bills. We are recreating an anachronistic debtor prison system whereby the poor are taken advantage of and turned into slaves. Not everyone can afford the increasing costs of living which means many simply can't pay off old debts. Whether it's because of general economic conditions, disability, unexpected medical expenses, car maintenance, or anything else doesn't matter, no one should be jailed for being poor. It's also the worst way for a debt collector to get their money because not only will the indebted individual no longer be working, once they're out it will be harder, if not impossible, to find someone willing to hire a former inmate. Unless, of course, the plan is to take advantage of said inmates and use them as cheap, disposable slave labor.

Any prison or judge allowing this practice should be punished and any persons incarcerated because of debt must be freed immediately, their record expunged, and paid compensation for their unlawful imprisonment. We must resist and make every instance of this legal perversion publicly known. We must support our fellows who experience injustice however we can. And we must vote for strong leaders willing to prosecute the system itself.

51 - Abolish For-Profit Private Prisons

Since the US prison population has grown so dramatically, it has become necessary for states to contract private businesses to house prisoners. Make no mistake, these are for profit prisons: they stipulate by contract that a certain head count must be maintained in order to remain open and for the state to not receive a fine. This produces an actual demand for prisoners and the supply is found through over policing and the War on Drugs. Judges increasingly give out maximum penalties to maintain prisoner head counts and some even receive kickbacks for each prisoner they send to a private facility. Making matters worse prisoners are often made to do physical labor or produce items for little or no pay creating a slave labor force in all but name.

Making profit from human misery is obscene and so is creating a demand for it. Private prisons must be shut down. There is no way they can be regulated where they don't create a demand for prisoners, or otherwise corrupt the legal system. Since these prisons came about because of overcrowding in actual prisons, we must lower the number of people in jail. Ending the War on Drugs and over-policing will sever supply chains for private prisons and dramatically lower the number of people in jail and within the broader penal system. Inmates in private prisons convicted of serious crimes should be transferred to state prisons and the rest should be released, pardoned, and compensated. Judges found to be enriching themselves, legislators who allowed this to happen, and those in charge of the private prison industry should be charged with conspiracy, human trafficking, then made to pay punitive damages and sentenced to lengthy prison stays if convicted.

52 - Abolish For-Profit Private Law Firms

The well-known and increasing wealth disparity in the US is a problem that extends beyond wealth and standards of living into the realm of basic equality under the law. Low-income individuals are incarcerated at disproportionally higher rates than higher income earners. The people responsible for the 2008 economic crash have never even seen the inside of the courtroom, let alone a prison sentence. Celebrities and the wealthy can afford the best lawyers who manage to get their clients reduced prison stays, or no jail time at all. Most everybody else can't afford legal aid and have little choice but to go with a public defender. However, public defenders are so overwhelmed with cases they can only spend minutes with each client and usually recommend taking a plea deal. By the time the trial date arrives most people just want an end to their various legal nightmares.

Private law firms have their own problems including the fact that their businesses first and they do everything possible to maximize profit. For most people private legal help is exclusionarily expensive and the very nature of private law firms for criminal cases creates and reinforces a caste system of people with different legal privileges.

The amount of money a person has should not determine their guilt, or their punishment.

This double standard equates people with lower incomes as second class citizens; it's a form of discrimination against the poor and a means of control. Our law makers and judges need to enforce the law equally regardless of wealth. The system of incarcerating the poor and letting the wealthy get off easy, or walk away scott-free must be put to an end. We are supposed to be equal under the law, but we can't be in a broken system where the quality of our rights is determined by our paychecks. We need to invest in public defenders by increasing their pay and decreasing their workloads by hiring more well-trained staff. We also need to abolish for-profit law firms because their existence expands class differences into the realm of the law. Without private firms everyone would need to use public defenders which would require us to invest in them by default. And if the wealthy couldn't hire private defenders they'd have a more vested interest in addressing the problems in our criminal justice system.

53 - Stop Indiscriminate Use Of "Non-Lethal" Weapons

Non-lethal weapons are meant to impede suspects and control large crowds of people without killing them. Unfortunately many of these weapons, while less lethal, can very much kill a person their potential for overuse is being fulfilled. Tasers, for instance, run the risk of causing heart attacks, but are used in mundane situations like routine traffic stops. New microwave weaponry is said to be non-lethal and safe, but if for some a reason a person becomes incapacitated and cannot get away from the invisible beam they can suffer serious injuries including their contacts fusing to their retinas, internal damage, and potentially death by microwave. Even bean bags and rubber bullets have the potential to kill especially if fired blindly upon a crowd. A person hit in the throat or head could sustain severe and deadly injuries. Because these weapons are "non-lethal" officers use them on a whim, on peaceful protestors, motorists, children, people with disabilities, basically whenever and on whomever they feel like. Officers routinely resort to using the weapons instead of even attempting deescalate a situation. While these weapons aren't as lethal as traditional guns and bullets, they still pose risks and should be used cautiously, sparingly, and only when a situation truly warrants their use.

This is one of many aspects that must be included in reforming law enforcement. Continuous training with a focus on de-escalation should be mandatory for all police officers. They also need to be trained how to identify and communicate with neuro-divergent individuals, the deaf, and other populations that may only utilize non-verbal communication. They need to be trained to truly protect and serve instead of treating every American like the enemy.

54 - Create Accountability For Police Officers

Police officers shoot family dogs for barking; tase and beat handcuffed suspects; tackle, body slam, and arrest school children; mace peaceful protestors; shoot unarmed black men for anything at all, and let others die while in their custody. When bad cops are being investigated for their reckless actions and violent, they're almost always investigated by their own department then given paid leave until said investigation concludes that the officers in question acted reasonably. On the rare occasions they do make it to trial. The legal system takes the word of any police officer over a regular citizen and the verdicts rendered are almost always not guilty. Statistics show that there's only a small amount of people who experience police brutality, but when it does the officers involved often face little or no consequences for their actions. While anyone can be the undeserving target of police brutality, blacks and minorities are disproportionally the targets and they know to fear the police.

Increased, or differently calibrated, psychological screenings can be used to eliminate at least some individuals from the hiring pool before they become problems. We must also institute civilian oversight for all police departments nationwide; no one else is allowed to investigate themselves for misconduct, why should police departments be any different? All on duty officers must wear at least two working body cams at all times and police vehicles must have two dash cams, one on the left and right side of the windshield. And we must always film them.

55 - End And Reverse Police Militarization

From big cities to rural farming communities, the United States militarized our police departments. After 9/11 police forces in large cities and small towns alike have been receiving military grade equipment and weapons which in the past had been reserved for SWAT teams. Armored transport vehicles, fully automatic weapons, accompanying military grade armor are all at the disposal of local PD's across the country. Military weapons are given to officers who, for the most part, have no military training and have no business using them. Individuals within the military have noticed officers' inappropriate handling of fully automatic weapons; pointing their weapons forward, finger on the trigger instead of downwards, finger beside the trigger until ready to fire. Just like their over and misuse traditional firearms and non-lethal weapons they continue the pattern by using military grade gear in unnecessary situations: common drug busts, the execution of search warrants, to crowd control. If a situation warrants extreme force we have specially trained officers in SWAT for these scenarios. The general public overwhelmingly disapproves of police militarization and it creates more fear than it does real, or perceived, safety from terrorists. There's no justifiable reason to have ordinary police officers equipped with military hardware.

We must therefore stop and reverse the militarization of our domestic police forces. We must require police departments sell their military grade equipment back to government, or destroy it. We must also prohibit both the use and acquisition of military equipment like armored transports and fully automatic weapons by domestic police departments in the future.

56 - Forbid The Use Of Advanced Surveillance Technologies

Police officers have devices to access cell phone data of individuals at routine traffic stops, or en masse. Mass surveillance techniques like these are used to illegally collect evidence against US citizens for various crimes often related to the possession or distribution of drugs. The evidence then undergoes "parallel construction," a process by which officers and prosecutors can pretend pieces of evidence were obtained by legal means. This throws probable cause and the need for warrants out the window; an entirely new form of illegal search and seizure via electronic means. Illegally obtained evidence from other mass surveillance programs and technologies are also responsible for putting people behind bars. To do this, they treat us all as potential suspects, rifle through our lives, and break the law themselves.

We can demand our leaders pass legislation to prevent this; however, existing laws are already being broken and we must hold those who violate our rights responsible for their actions. We must require our representatives to muster the political will and courage to prosecute the offenders to the fullest extent of the law and prevent further erosion of our rights. As much as politicians love saying how much they love the Constitution, their actions are speaking far more loudly. They can forget the rhetoric and act on those beliefs, resign, or be removed by voters. If the police are breaking the law as they often do, it means they cannot be trusted and simply should not be permitted to utilize certain technologies at all.

57 - End Racist Sentencing

The US does not have liberty and justice for all,
rather liberty and justice for different people in different
amounts. Despite people of color being a minority of the
population, they make up the bulk of the prison population;
receive harsher sentences and lengthier prison terms. Our
legal system itself is a key pillar in modern institutional
racism and slavery.

Racist sentencing is yet another reason we require
our police and even our courts to be policed. While people
who commit crimes, regardless of race, should not go
unpunished, they should all receive the same punishment. If
any two prisoners are convicted of the same crime they
should have the same sentences, and should any inmate
find themselves serving a longer sentence than another
inmate for the same crime, the longer of the two sentences
must be immediately reduced and equalized to the other. If
an inmate finds themselves having already served longer
than another inmate for the same crime then said inmate
must be liberated and compensated for their wrongful
incarceration. Police must also stop targeting people based
on the color of their skin, or racial profiling. Our current
laws against discrimination are clearly not enough. We
must therefore enact stronger legislation, police the police,
and continue combatting institutional racism. Furthermore
civilian oversight needs to be permitted to investigate
judges, individual officers, and their departments should
allegations of racist behavior surface. Those individuals
should then be punished if a clear pattern of discrimination
can be shown and the punishments of individuals sentenced
with prejudice rectified.

58 - Implement Criminal Justice Reform

We have a legal system, not a justice system and it
doles out unjust punishments unreflecting the nature of
crimes committed; creates systematic disparities in
sentencing along racial and class lines; incarcerates non-

violent drug users longer than some rapists, murders, and child molesters; focuses on punitive measures over rehabilitation; leaves individuals in solitary confinement for years inflicting long term psychological damage on them; and it holds violent criminals and non-violent ones together. Our contemporary model of corrections is essentially a model for a university in crime: when non-violent criminals are mixed with dangerous criminals the non-violent offenders leave prison with higher likelihoods of recidivism and escalation. It's also a disservice to the victims of other far more serious transgressions.

Our laws must be reformed both at state and national levels so punishments fit the crimes. We cannot allow rapists and murders to go free while we make more room growing numbers of non-violent offenders. Prisons that focus on rehabilitation see lower rates of violent incidents within the jail and lower rates of recidivism once inmates leave jail. The same is true for jails that do not cohouse violent and non-violent inmates. We must also abolish mandatory minimums and three-strike laws. Either our lawmakers reform the law or we must find a way to reform it for them.

59 - Improve Prison Quality

Prisons in the US are overcrowded, underfunded, and made more dangerous by these and many other problems. Overcrowding, increasing violence, sexual assault, poor sanitation, poor nutrition, poor medical treatment, and overall mistreatment- which is often directed at minorities and disabled people- are all common issues across the country. While some may argue those convicted of the worst kinds of crime deserve this treatment, it is against the law and US Constitution and we must uphold the law of the land. It should also be noted that most prisoners are not violent offenders, and some have been wrongly convicted. These are examples of abuse and neglect, not justice.

These injustices should be corrected by addressing many of the issue above and by insisting upon greater prison reforms. Ending the War on Drugs, over policing, and mandatory minimums will reduce the number of inmates dramatically thus alleviating the issue of overcrowding. It's more productive and compassionate to focus on rehabilitation instead of punitive imprisonment. Only a very small percentage of people can never be let back out to rejoin society, the overwhelming majority of them can and will be released one day. Instead of creating an environment which breeds destructive behavior we must create an environment conducive to reforming criminals: violent and non-violent offenders should not be lumped together ; the psychological torture of solitary confinement must be abolished; and prisons need to have enough funding for proper sanitation and facility maintenance. Through a combination of activism, legislation, and civilian inspections we can achieve a better prison system where human beings are not treated like animals and where the punishments fit the crimes.

60 - Abolish The Death Penalty

The United States still practices cruel and unusual punishment every time it sentences someone to death. Most states where state sponsored executions are allowed utilize lethal injection as the method for inducing death. However, hearing the horror stories of lethal injection inmates on death row will opt for the electric chair if it's an option. Lethal injection is described as torturous, like drowning while being on fire. No medical expertise is present in its design or implementation because doctors refuse to break their Hippocratic oaths by assisting executions in any way. As a result, the drug cocktail injected fails to do as originally intended (act as an anesthetic) and the procedure itself can take multiple attempts when untrained workers can't find, or keep missing a vein.

Death by electrocution fills the execution chamber with the smell of burning meat, induces violent spasms, causes parts of the body to begin smoking, produces intense pain, and like lethal injection is not always effective the first time around.

All means of execution come with similar problems, but means is secondary to the fact that we don't always execute the right person. While a wrongly incarcerated person cannot get their time served back they can, at least in theory, be given a second chance if exonerated. There are no second chances for exonerated corpses.

Because state sanctioned killing does little if anything to deter violent crime, costs taxpayers more per year to keep someone on death row than merely incarcerating them, constitutes cruel and unusual punishment, and removes any chances at rehabilitation or exoneration the death penalty should be abolished and relegated to history books. Some may argue those who are sentenced to die and are guilty of their crimes deserve their fate which may be true, however if that is indeed the case then a lifetime in a prison cell would better serve justice.

Government

61 - Encourage Community

"See something? Say something," is an establishment slogan meant to help catch terrorists, but only heightens paranoia and encourages neighbors to spy on each other. Created for the Department of Homeland Security by an advertising company the phrase is printed in public spaces for all to see. The Nazis and other authoritarian regimes throughout history encouraged a similar mentality in order to breed loyalty to the state, or party and control dissent. Well intentioned or not, it's a symptom of society long consumed by, perhaps obsessed with, fear. This cultural change is even physically embedded in our houses: during the first half of 20th century houses were built with decks and porches in the front yard facing the street creating a more open atmosphere and sense of community. Now, they're usually built with these features in the back, away from the road, private and secluded from the rest of the world. With each generation turning more inward and becoming more suspicious we've reached a point where loneliness is recognized as a mental health epidemic. Humans are social creatures and biologically require social interactions to remain healthy.

Instead of fostering suspicion and fear, we should be encouraging the return communities that have a real sense of community about them. When neighbors know each other and talk with each other it becomes much harder for a terrorist or criminal, to hide. Bringing back a sense of community would also combat the loneliness epidemic. Instead of displaying paranoid catch phrases something like "Greet your neighbors" would be more effective. Strong community bonds have profound psychological benefits and reduce crime. The best and most direct solution to this problem is of course to simply talk with our neighbors.

62 - Reform The Legislative Process

Modern legislation can be so long that their length is weaponized by ensuring no one has time to read certain bills in their entirety. Members of Congress are forced to vote for legislation blindly while simultaneously adding riders and amendments pertaining to issues completely unrelated to the bills on which they're attached. Riders are used to pass laws that wouldn't pass by themselves but stand a better chance when hidden within thousands of pages of text. Riders are also used as poison pills to sabotage legislation by including outrageous provisions that usually defeat the purpose of the proposed bill.

First, we must force Congress to place a moratorium on all riders; anything that should be including in a bill should be included during its drafting. Members of Congress must, like school children, be required to do their reading assignments and they must be allotted enough time reasonably do so. This reading requirement further mandates that bills be limited in length so that the time needed to read any given bill remains reasonable.

63 - Require Subject Literacy In Congress

The US education system is in poor shape to say the least. However, this problem doesn't end with students, but endemic ignorance is demonstrated by many of our leaders on what feels like a daily, sometimes hourly, basis. For instance, climate change: a reality that's already here and getting worse is controversial and politicized. Almost every scientist and academic institution agrees that climate change is real and human activities are responsible for its rapid pace. But there are still a lot of people who deny this reality even when temperature and severe weather records break in front of their eyes every year. Not to mention much of the more complicated data gathered from satellites and computer simulations of the climate are easily available online. This issue relates back to how we perceive education and intellect in general. Too often is intelligence mocked and ignored when it should be praised and listened to. We must change our attitudes towards intelligence and ignorance. Informed opinions are indeed superior to uninformed opinions. We must lower our tolerance of ignorance especially from those in power.

Members of Congress who continually show ignorance of scientific matters yet sit on committees concerning scientific matters should be forced off those committees or forced to resign from Congress altogether. Members of Congress have demonstrated a lack of scientific understanding on matters of global climate change and even basic human biology- particularly female anatomy- yet despite their ignorance they still shape the policies that directly impact these matters of concern. This ignorance isn't limited to scientific matters, but basic US history and even the contents of the Constitution. It is at best a national embarrassment. It's disgusting and mass-homicide at worst. Policies created by inaccurate information costs lives: severe weather exacerbated by human climate change costs lives; women's health legislation set by ignorant old men costs lives; food and drug safety requirements drafted by food and drug company executives instead of doctors and nutritionists costs lives; and the same can be said of any other policy matter crafted by proud, willful ignorance.

We must not only vote for well-informed candidates, but if there is a lack of well-informed candidates it is our responsibility to find them and convince them to run for office. It should also be made standard policy that any member of Congress participating in any matter must demonstrate at least a working knowledge of the subject at hand. There is no place for ignorance of this magnitude in running a country or forming its legislation and it cannot be tolerated any longer.

64 - Eliminate Big Money In Politics

Money is considered speech which leaves everybody voiceless, except for the wealthiest among us. Supreme Court decisions like Citizens United- the most famous of many decisions- allow money to be considered free speech. It's not free speech however; it is the legalization of bribery: individuals and corporations can donate unlimited, undisclosed amounts of money to political campaigns. It also disenfranchises everyone who's not a multimillionaire, or billionaire; it deprioritizes the will of the people, allowing it to be usurped by the will of the mega-wealthy. This is not a democracy; it's not even a republic. It's an oligarchy. Legislation is drafted and passed with the best interest of campaign contributors in mind, not what's best for the people.

The Supreme Court's decision on Citizens United must be overturned. We can make a legal case for class discrimination and sue the US Government: equating money to speech means most of us have no voice because use our free speech on food and rent. We can also enact new laws targeting our system of legalized corruption like capping the total amount of money any political campaign may spend on behalf of a candidate; limiting the amount of money a campaign can spend on advertising; and creating a 15% tax on all campaign funds.

65 - Break The Revolving Door

The revolving door plagues our system of government and cannot be tolerated any longer. It's one of the mechanisms by which special interests control our legislative process and refers to the unscrupulous practice of legislators becoming lobbyists and vice versa. CEO's, business owners, and financial stakeholders become members of Congress then regulate their own industries. When their term is up, they become lobbyists to influence their replacements. Direct conflicts of interest are both legal and financially rewarded by our current system.

Public officials cannot be trusted to recuse themselves from legislative positions with conflicts of interest. They must be called out. Any existing laws forbidding conflict of interests must be enforced and new laws created explicitly prohibiting this practice. No one shall be permitted to become a member of any legislative body if they are, or have ever been, significantly financially linked to an industry requiring regulation by the legislative body they seek to become a member of.

66 - Improve The Accuracy Of Our Representation

Our so called representatives in Congress are, more often than not, not representative of us. The majority of Congress is male. About half of them are millionaires. No demographic is accurately represented in Congress. Millionaires and billionaires don't know how much a gallon of milk costs, let alone have any inkling of what it's like to perpetually struggle from paycheck to paycheck. These people have no business setting policies and very likely can't fathom the needs of working people. We need accurate representation, not entitled, self-serving aristocrats. Our political process is further complicated by the two party system that has entrenched itself into the fabric of our government making it nearly impossible for third-party candidates to run a successful campaign.

First and foremost we must make better voting decisions at the poles, but that's difficult when only millionaires are able to successfully run for office. Public pressure can demand candidates refuse donations from corporate sponsors and then codify it into law. We must also undo decades of gerrymandering by redrawing districts impartially and require future redistricting be done by an impartial civilian experts in demographics, statistics, and other relevant fields. At the very least elected officials cannot be allowed to draw the districts that get them elected, which essentially lets officials chose their voters instead of voters choosing their officials. We must reform our system and institute proportional representation allowing any party with a certain percentage of the population to have a proportional amount of seats in Congress. And of course, more of us should consider running for office ourselves, or contributing time and skills to campaigns we support. We can also utilize social media and grassroots strategies to win seats and affect change from within.

67 - Abolish The Electoral College

The Electoral College is a remnant of slavery and appointed two of the last three presidents against the popular will of the people. It makes the power of a single vote worth different amounts in different states because in this system states with the largest populations are underrepresented and smaller states are overrepresented. A popular example illustrating this fact is that California has one elector for every 700,000 people, roughly; however, Wyoming has one elector for about every 200,000 people. One of the most basic principles of a democracy or republic is that individual votes must all be equal in weight. Some people argue the Electoral College ensures that presidential candidates don't ignore the smaller states, but this fear is unfounded and in reality it disenfranchises tens of millions of voters. Or phrased another way, the Electoral College is systemic voter suppression and states that have the most voters are penalized for having the most voters.

Abolishing the Electoral College is a necessity for American democracy and can be done without altering the Constitution. While a Constitutional Amendment creating a direct democracy isn't necessarily an imperative it's still worthy of pursuit. The Constitution is the law of the land and equally as important is its significance in American culture: though not divine in nature it's treated as sacred text, at least rhetorically, and changing it to create a direct democracy would be powerful legislatively and culturally. However, we can also pressure Congress and individual states to adopt legislation mandating that Electoral votes automatically go to the winner of the national popular vote. Removing the Electoral College, or negating it legislatively, will make all votes count equally creating fairer elections that better reflect the will of the people. It may also have the added benefits of increasing voter turnout and making it easier for third-party candidates to successfully enter the race.

68 - Enact Austerity Measures For Congress

Members of Congress hold our government hostage for politics and are doing so more often. In 2013 the government shutdown delayed federal emergency aid to areas of the country experiencing severe flooding. The longest government shutdown in history forced economic hardships on 800,000 furloughed employees: many needed to visit food banks; received eviction notices; while others like TSA workers and air traffic controllers continued working without pay. Fully employed people couldn't afford food, rent, heat, or anything else because a small number of individuals wanted to play politics with people's lives. Congress threatens the wellbeing of millions of Americans whenever they try to take away healthcare away, or refuse to raise the minimum wage. Members of Congress enjoy some of the best healthcare in the world; give themselves raises; keep getting paid during shutdowns, and it's all supplied by our taxes. The levels of entitlement and hypocrisy displayed by certain members of our Congress are the unacceptable status-quo.

Given these hypocrisies we must require Congress to finally feel some austerity measures. Their pay should be tied to an open government; if the government shuts down and federal employees are made to work without pay then members of Congress will too. Congressional salaries should be equal to the federal minimum wage and their healthcare should be whatever a typical minimum wage earner can afford. It's unjust that our representatives are so well compensated for making it harder for families to put food on the table or see a doctor.

69 - Increase Veterans Benefits

On any given night in the middle of winter almost 40,000 veterans find themselves' homeless and over 20,000 of them are unsheltered. Post-Traumatic Stress Disorder afflicts over half to two-thirds of homeless veterans. Twenty veterans commit suicide every day. This is a national embarrassment: those who serve their country deserve to be served by their country and not discarded like broken tools. Congress allocates trillions of dollars to fight political wars and on superfluous military projects, but cannot provide sufficient care for the soldiers risking their lives and come home missing limbs if at all. When trying to use their benefits those who return from the battlefield are often met with red tape, administrative errors, systemic inefficiency, and subsequent delays and denials. Why should anyone fight for a country whose leaders are unwilling to fight for them on a battlefield of words and paperwork?

Our soldiers require higher pay and more comprehensive benefits. A mental health infrastructure should be created consisting of numerous facilities staffed with trained psychologists, psychiatrists, and therapists. A post-deployment sense of community is also important and attainable through programs like group therapy, or optional communal housing. Furthermore the entire Department of Veterans Affairs needs to upgrade both their physical structures along with their digital services and records. The VA also requires increased funding and staffing for current day to day operations.

70 - Relax Voter ID Laws

Strict voter ID laws restrict legal citizens from voting. The arguments in favor of increasingly strict voter identification laws claim it's to prevent voter fraud, but the kind of voter impersonation that these laws aim to combat is so rare as to be almost nonexistent. In practice however, voters are refused the right to vote especially those belonging to minority populations which belies the racist intentions motivating this type of draconian legislation.

People should be encouraged and assisted to vote if need be. Various forms of ID, not just state issued driver's licenses should be accepted at the voting booth. Requiring specific identification creates bureaucratic hurdles for voters and is in effect no different from a poll tax.

71 - Overhaul The Immigration System

The United States is and always has been a nation of immigrants. Despite the sheer number and scope of our problems we're still considered the land of opportunity where people can create a better life for themselves. The Statue of Liberty stands as a welcoming colossus and the embodiment of our proclaimed ideals, but we have yet to live up to them. Throughout our history immigrants have been met with prejudice, mistrust, and alienation. They're demonized as rapists, murders, and drug dealers despite all evidence indicting exactly the opposite: documented or not, immigrants commit crimes at significantly lower rates than native born citizens. Immigrants are also a crucial part of our economy working tens of millions of jobs many of which most Americans are unwilling to do. Most undocumented workers want to be citizens someday and to that end they pay billions of dollars in taxes and even file tax returns every year. Despite these and other benefits of immigration like utilizing international talent and brain power we fearfully keep trying to wall ourselves off from the greater world and its people. The immigration process itself is purposefully riddled with ethnic quotas, restrictions, exceedingly long application periods, and prohibitive, nonrefundable expenses.

If we want to live up to our ideals and reap the economic benefits of doing so we need to overhaul the entire immigration. At the very least the government should stop charging potential citizens money for their applications and remove xenophobic, archaic quotas from the process entirely. The costs need to be further reduced if not made entirely free for potential citizens considering hundreds of millions of people around the world are lucky to be making dollars a day. Our current immigration rules and regulations need to be made user friendly, streamlined and designed in a way to make citizenship more attainable for those who seek it, not more restrictive. The merits making an individual worthy of citizenship do not include their race, ethnicity, religion, or class and it's long overdue our laws reflect this truth.

72 - Abolish ICE

ICE is relatively new agency created in 2003 as part of reactionary post 9/11 legislation that exchanges civil liberties for the illusion of security. The creation of Immigration and Customs Enforcement, or ICE, as part of the Department of Homeland Security makes it clear that the United States considers immigrants as potential threat to national security, equating them with terrorists and increasingly treating them as such. ICE is responsible for brutally detaining people, separating families, and maintaining modern day internment camps. The general practice of deporting people for being undocumented is inhumane and often a death sentence. Being undocumented is a civil misdemeanor akin to public intoxication or petty theft and the process of having their entire life uprooted, being detained and then shipped away is wildly unequal punishment. The people being deported are ordinary, hardworking individuals that have usually already been living in the country for a number of years without incident and have created families and ties to local communities. ICE is further police militarization and acts more like the Gestapo hunting Jews than a legitimate law enforcement agency.

The solution is clear, ICE must be abolished along with the practice of deportation for misdemeanors. Immigration responsibilities should be transferred under the jurisdiction of the Department of Health and Human Services and in the event an undocumented immigrant also happens to be a serious criminal we have police agencies to deal with those situations already.

73 - Enact Common Sense Gun Control Legislation

One of the most, if not the most, seemingly

controversial issues facing the country as of this writing is gun control. The U.S. has more mass shootings than any other first world nation. Tens of thousands of people die from gun related incidents every year. Freedom isn't free and the cost of the freedom protected by the Second Amendment is tens of thousands of lives annually. Congress refuses to enact legislation regulating firearms supported by an overwhelming majority of the American people and have made it clear they value the financial support of the NRA than they do an honest interpretation of "well regulated Militia" and the lives school children.

There are a lot of arguments for and against any kind of firearm related legislation, but the simple fact is over 90% of Americans support universal background checks; 81% support raising the purchasing age of firearms to 21; 84% support banning sales of firearms to anyone convicted of a violent crime like domestic abuse.

Preventing all gun related deaths may never happen, but just as automobile related deaths haven't been abolished, the regulations keep many dangerous drivers off the road and save lives. Unfortunately, the NRA has ceased being a mere safety organization and association of gun owners. Instead, it has mutated into a powerful political entity which uses its money to buy the allegiance of senators and representatives in order to create a tyranny of the minority on this issue – and most important protect gun sales. To defeat them voters must actually preform the inglorious and mundane task of calling their representatives repeatedly and often. But with persistent, albeit rather ordinary, action extraordinary changes can be made and this is true for any issue.

74 - Create Term Limits For Judges

Unlike the Supreme Court, lower district courts have elected, instead of appointed judges. Superficially it looks harmless, but a system with judges seeking reelection have unintended consequences often undermining the rule of law. Judges beholden to constituents are more susceptible to the pressures of popular opinion and therefore to being compelled to cast verdicts, or punishments, they might not have otherwise. If constituents believe a judge is being too lenient said judge may begin giving out more maximum sentences to undeserving criminals, or conversely if a judge is seen as being too harsh may begin giving out more lenient sentences to equally, but oppositely undeserving criminals. Judicial elections are also subject to the unsavory influences of corporate campaign contributors like any other current election.

Judges and their rulings should not be beholden to the whims of public opinion, but should instead base their rulings on their own soundness of judgement. Requiring judges only serve a single term and restricting life terms to 20 years would attenuate the conflict of interest for judges between preforming their duties and keeping their approval ratings up. Big Money also needs to be excised from judicial politics by limiting the amount any candidate can receive from any single individual and in total.

75 - Respect Sovereignty Of Tribal Nations

The indigenous people of North America have called the continent home for over 10,000 years when mammoths grazed besides receding glaciers at the end of the last Ice Age. Territories still held by indigenous tribes today are closer to sovereign nations than they are to US states. To this day the United States government breaks formal treaties, official diplomatic agreements, with sovereign Native American Tribes. After centuries of genocide and institutionalized acculturation the remaining indigenous populations struggle with high levels of poverty and they're rights to self-governance are being legislated away. The federal government assists corporations building pipelines through native lands and rivers; leaks commonly poison the land and water people depend on; all while breaking tribal laws in the process.

For the sake of justice we must finally start respecting the rights and lives of indigenous people around the world starting here at home. Tribal sovereignty needs to be respected and upheld. Individual states can step up and refuse to send law enforcement agents or National Guard members to enforce illegal actions perpetrated against Tribal Nations. We must pressure our representatives to fight for indigenous people and their rights; cease and repeal legislation attempting to undermine said people and rights; support the inclusion of Tribal Nations in the United Nations; return unoccupied land stolen from broken treaties and provide compensation for lands occupied with residential populations. Furthermore Tribal Nations should be permitted to use force if necessary to defend their lands from illegal seizure and occupation.

76 - Reduce Defense Spending

The US spends more than China, Saudi Arabia, Russia, The United Kingdom, India, France, and Japan combined on its defense budget. Over 50% of discretionary funding -hundreds of billions of dollars- is allocated to the military. And yet, American veterans go without their earned benefits and make up a sizable fraction of our nation's homeless population. Other programs go without funding because "we can't afford it," yet, we can always afford trillions of dollars on endless wars.

We can more than afford to shrink our military budget by a considerable sum and still remain the strongest, most technologically advanced military in the world. That money can then be reallocated to other areas that are in desperate need of attention like the nation's failing infrastructure, public education, and most appropriately taking care of veterans. The military budget must be shrunk and wasteful programs especially must be cut. Beyond what Congress can do and should have already done, we must also pressure the defense contractors that make up the military industrial complex to stop selling technologies that don't work; stalling projects for more grant money; and stop pushing for unnecessary wars.

77 - End Drone Programs

The United States is waging asymmetrical warfare with its unmanned drones against largely civilian populations in numerous countries throughout the Middle

East. War is a video game played on screen but the people killed are not polygons and pixels. There's no accountability for pilots or officers who mistakenly or purposefully attack civilian targets or areas where collateral damage is a certainty. Slaying innocent people is a war of terror responsible for enflaming anti-American sentiment and creating new terrorists. The use of military drones domestically for surveillance purposes by law enforcement is also majorly under-regulated by both federal and state legislation. Wherever they are, whatever they're doing, drones are also susceptible to hacking.

Drone programs need to be brought to an end. Oversight of the military drone program is a power Congress already possesses, but allows continuing and escalating attacks in civilian dense areas. Congress is therefore complicit and cannot be tasked with ongoing oversight, instead we must demand of a necessary majority in the House and Senate to pass a bill decommissioning our current drone programs and forbidding their use in the future. States legislatures must also pass laws forbidding the use of military drones domestically; forbidding any kind of arms on domestic drones; and forbidding the inclusion of advanced surveillance technologies.

78 - Stop Endless, Illegal Regime Change Wars

It is an undeniable fact that the United States is the greatest threat to world peace: responsible for crimes against humanity and war profiteering, the vast majority of American military operations inflict terror around the world. We're told these wars are necessary to defend our freedoms and spread democracy yet the countries occupied by US forces pose no substantial threat and the US supports most of the world's dictatorships. These oil profiteering conflicts where we ignore the sovereignty of other nations are illegal by our own Constitutional laws and international laws.

For the sake of lives and world peace our endless, illegal regime change wars need to finally be stopped. We must pressure both the legislative and executive branches to withdraw our troops. Ceasing drone strikes and destroying the military industrial complex are also necessary avenues for achieving peace. Furthermore, individuals influencing foreign policy while making money from investments in oil, or defense contracting companies have sold out their country and should be tried to corruption and treason.

79 - Hold Administrations Accountable For War Crimes

The United States is responsible for aiding and committing war crimes, crimes against humanity, and breaking other international laws. Leaving tens of thousands of civilians dead in Pakistan; tens of thousands more in Afghanistan; hundreds of thousands in Iraq is what the US calls liberation. We sell weapons to authoritarian nations and rebel factions within them; we topple legitimate governments and support most of the world's dictatorships. Little accountability exists for individual service members who commit atrocities and none exists for government officials, presidents and their administrations, or anyone else with the power to authorize, order, and orchestrate illegal wars, regime changes, selling weapons to be used in war crimes, war profiteering, and other foreign policy decisions cost millions of lives around the world. We also make ourselves less safe by spending unimaginable resources to essentially create new enemies.

We need to create a system of accountability for top officials. Civilian oversight and increased transparency are necessities. We can recognize the limited jurisdictions of the International Criminal Court located at The Hague in the Netherlands. Doing so would make potentially make it easier to try American officials for violations of human rights and breaking international laws. Domestic courts can be used to sue administrations for various transgressions like fraud, conspiracy to commit fraud, man slaughter, and reckless endangerment. Administrations concoct narratives to convince the public we need to go war; narratives that just aren't true and they know it. Based on fabrications people are sent to places where it's a certainty some will not make it back in one piece, or at all. Furthermore, these actions are arguably unconstitutional and treasonous: our ongoing wars do not have Congressional approval and they exchange human lives and our national security to help make private corporations massive profits.

80 - Disarm Nuclear Stockpiles

The United States alone has enough nuclear weapons to destroy the world several times over. At the same time the stockpile of thousands of warheads relies on antiquated technology and lackadaisical security and training as a number of guards fall asleep, order pizzas, and even cheat on their application exams. And from time to time we lose track of one of them. Maintaining thousands of nuclear devices costs millions of dollars every year and their very existence creates the possibility of an apocalyptic nuclear holocaust.

Disarming our nuclear arsenal is a necessary step towards world peace. No nuclear armed nation wants to be the first to disarm, but one of them must. The United States taking that step would send a powerful message around the world and likely encourage others to do the same. With every device we disarm we decrease the risk of both an accident occurring and annihilation.

81 - Demand Disclosure

Many Americans and people around the world have seen objects in the sky that defy the known laws of aerodynamics and physics in general. Hundreds, if not thousands, of documented eyewitness reports, photographs, and videos exist of unidentified flying objects, or UFO's. A number of sightings are confirmed by radar and even occasionally physical evidence like elevated radiation levels and debris. Whether extraterrestrial in origin or classified military technology, the existence of this extraordinary phenomenon compels us to ask the questions "how do they work and what powers them?" which urgently demand answers. Whatever technology is being utilized likely has the capacity to change our understanding of the universe and eliminate our dependence of fossil fuels.

We must therefore demand complete disclosure of any and all classified information regarding the subject of UFO's. The questions need to be asked at political debates and the conversation moved into the mainstream where it can garner awareness and support. Filing requests under the Freedom of Information Act incessantly from the public and elected officials will further increase pressure on the powers that be. Independent research also needs to be done in an attempt understand the technology observed by witnesses and the experiments must to be streamed live on the internet ensuring it cannot be sequestered away. Demonstrating UFO technology to the world would likely force governments to disclose their knowledge of the phenomenon if they seek to continue controlling the narrative in any way.

Economy and Wealth Inequality

81 - End Initial Job Applications Asking About Convictions

One in every one hundred Americans is part of the penal system and it's difficult to near impossible for them to find a job. In other words, there's a segment of the population that is capable and willing to work, but are not given the opportunity. Most people convicted of a crime are non-violent offenders deserving of a chance to better their lives and leaving a swathe of the population out of work is detriment to the economy, a disservice to those who have served their time, and increases the likelihood of recidivism. Eliminating some of the barriers preventing former inmates from finding employment would be boon for the economy and help keep people from returning to jail.

Applications inevitably ask about criminal history and anyone checking the box indicating they have record is just not going to be considered for a position. Job applications should thus remove the question. Employers, of course, can run background checks on potential employees, or inquire themselves later in the interview process. Such a small change will give millions of people the chance to get their foot in the door, the chance to make a first impression, and thus a better chance of finding a job. Even changing the question to ask about convictions for violent crimes would make a difference.

82 - Forgive Student Loan Debt

Millions of adults across the country are suffocating under oppressive debt. The average student loan debt is nearly $40,000 with steep interest rates and many individuals are simply unable to pay it back and unable to find financial security until they do. College tuition costs keep rising and they're predatory in nature by taking advantage of young people trying to better themselves. Students are pressured by teachers, parents, and society in general to go to college when they graduate high school at 18 and do not fully understand the weight of the debt they'll be taking on. And universities are perfectly happy to raise tuition to make profit off of hardworking students. The debt strangling a generation of Americans along with other contemporary economic pressures are compelling people to take their own lives to avoid living life as an indentured servant and the economic repercussions stemming from millions of people unable fully participate in the economy are already being felt beyond the student debt circle.

The only way to bring peace of mind to these millions of Americans and to stifle the fallout from a generation beginning their adult lives with less than nothing is to forgive all student loan debts regardless if an individual attained a diploma or not. Forgiving student loan debt will is a necessity that will stimulate the economy and save lives.

83 - Fund Social Safety Nets

Millions of Americans are only a single unexpected expense away from homelessness: a car problem, a serious medical issue, or myriad unforeseeable events. Most Americans have little or no savings. Financial stress and poverty are literally killing people every day: some take their own lives, some freeze to death in the middle of a city, and everyone's life expectancy is lessened by a lifetime of unfruitful labor.

Current social safety net programs should thus be bolstered and reformed in such a way as to reflect the economic reality facing growing numbers of Americans including children and the elderly. Funding for these programs can be secured from corporations if they are made to actually pay taxes and no longer receive subsidies. Expanding social programs and helping more Americans become financially stable will add hundreds of millions, perhaps billions of dollars into the economy by allowing more Americans to make larger asset purchases like new homes, or cars, or a much deserved vacation.

84 - Make Minimum Wage A Thriving Wage

The current minimum wage in the United States, when adjusted for inflation, is less than what minimum wage workers made fifty years ago. Most Americans are living paycheck to paycheck and make $30k a year or less. Living costs are always rising and millions of full-time employees are only a sick day's distance away from homelessness. With the exception of CEO's, wages are stagnant across almost all fields of employment despite ever increasing productivity and profits. Financial security remains elusive for many and instead of struggle for a lifetime of indentured servitude to student loans, rising rent, and manufactured scarcity these bleak economic prospects push increasing numbers of people to commit suicide. Furthermore, the only reason the push for a $15 minimum wage is making progress is because it is already too little too late.

Justice and human dignity require nothing less than a thriving wage tied to inflation and beginning immediately at $25 an hour and scheduled incremental increases to $40 an hour over the course of several years. Such a large increase would likely be too much for local, small businesses and should be granted government subsidies (as they already subsidize billion dollar industries) to meet these requirements. Another step must be the permanent bonding between profit and employee wages: the more profit a company makes then so too must the employees make more either in the form of raises and or bonuses.

85 - End Homelessness And Its Criminalization

The fact that homelessness exists at in the most prosperous nation on the planet is disgraceful and a societal failure. The hardships for people with nowhere to live are compounded by the prevalence of ordinances essentially criminalizing homelessness. Because the presence of street beggars reduce tourism and property values and because as a society we hold profit as more precious than human wellbeing and dignity we see authorities doing whatever they can to rid themselves of local homeless populations, everything except addressing the root causes of the problem. Local and state laws across the country prohibit giving food or money to panhandlers under the pretenses of public safety. If someone is causing a public safety hazard we already have laws to deal with that. Public spaces are filled with curved benches to make sleeping on them uncomfortable and difficult; spikes are erected under bridges to deprive them of shelter.

Homelessness also causes healthcare costs for all of us to go up: unable to afford health insurance, the homeless have no choice but to avoid doctors and hospitals until they need an emergency room where the expenses increase with severity. And they will often find themselves in the ER to begin with because living exposed to the elements without proper nutrition predisposes them to ailments more than people with a roof, food, and the ability to see a doctor for a checkup. Obviously, bills incurred by a homeless individual are likely to go unpaid for some time. Costs go up at every step of the cycle and is actually cheaper to just give everyone health coverage and a home.

The absurdity of modern homelessness is highlighted by the fact there are more vacant homes in the US than there homeless individuals and will be seen by future generations how we look back on working conditions in factories at the turn of the last century: primitive and exploitative. The very least we can do is fight every law and ordinance that penalizes the homeless for actions like panhandling and loitering. You cannot help someone to rebuild their life with fines and arrests; to the contrary it makes it immensely more difficult. But we can do more than that. We can eradicate homeless by expanding social safety nets, enacting universal health care, and universal housing programs. We have both fiscal and moral reason to end homeless, but more importantly we have the ability.

86 - Implement Universal Basic Income

Americans are struggling every day to make ends meet as the gap between rich and poor continues to grow. The costs of living are incessantly increasing, but pay rates do not increase with them. Poverty is very real in the United States: children are starving and people are dying of treatable medical conditions; less extreme, but equally as important and potentially as lethal, are long term effects of poverty induced on problems health, life expectancy, and cognitive development. A child cannot properly develop if they're malnourished and adults are killing themselves because of financial despair.

The growing hopelessness and ongoing hardships of Americans deserve resolutions. Therefore, every legal adult should receive an income to meet their basic needs. This policy will save lives and improve the quality of life for hundreds of millions of Americans. Detractors argue universal basic income would encourage laziness, but to contrary, experimental programs tried around the world have found when people are more financially stable they're happier, healthier, more productive, and more entrepreneurial.

87 - Implement Universal Basic Assets

The detrimental and life threatening impacts of poverty are clear, but even with an increase in the minimum wage and universal basic income individuals are still required to be a pawn in someone else's game, to make somebody else's profit. People will still be tied to their jobs, at the mercy of their managers and market forces in order to fully participate -and further be dependent upon- an unsustainable consumer economy. These actions, though positive, are not enough for individuals to gain a sense of self-sufficiency and independent.

All adult individuals need to have a stake in the economy and the means to supply their own basic needs. People require assets that can sustain them independently of economic crises, missing work because of illness, and eventually retirement. Homes and land are sitting vacant across the country that could be and should be used as new assets for millions of people. Other basic assets can come in the form of part ownership of state owned enterprises so when those companies make money so does everybody else.

88 - Legally Differentiate Between Corporations And People

Legally speaking, corporations are people: they are afforded the same basic rights as individuals and subject to the same laws. Corporations have far greater resources available to them than any individual and cannot be sentenced to jail time or given the death penalty for their crimes and thus have no standing for being entitled to the same protections as actual people. Defining corporations as people allows powerful individuals running corporations to receive the financial benefits of destroying our habitat; poisoning our air, land, food, and water; exploiting vulnerable populations around the world; and all other manner of predatory business practices without consequence. It also gives corporations the right to free speech allowing the people hiding behind them to funnel mountains of money into all manner of political campaigns and organizations to influence elections and legislation thereafter. The largest corporations in the world are more powerful than most countries. This is oligarchy with a veneer of democracy.

Corporations are managed by people and are nothing more. As such they have no business in politics or claiming rights of any kind. They cannot speak to legislation, they cannot donate to political campaigns, or organizations, and legislation allowing otherwise must be repealed, or overwritten by new legislation. Those who manage corporations must bear the full brunt of the consequences for devastating our planet, endangering the long-term survival of our species, and other undeniable transgressions.

89 - Create A New Tax Code

The United States is considered a tax haven abroad because of its complicated and lengthy tax code intentionally filled with endless loopholes that are nearly impossible to close. The immense length of our tax legislation benefits the wealthy by making it difficult to recognize unscrupulous structures embedded within the law and by making it difficult for anyone but tax experts to understand in its entirety. Furthermore, it's only the wealthy who can afford to take advantage of most tax schemes since most require surplus wealth that can be parted with while it moves around the system to multiply into more wealth. Individuals and families living paycheck to paycheck do not have surplus wealth nor time to part with the little wealth they have.

The current tax code does not work for the vast majority of Americans and needs to be entirely replaced with a straightforward and easily accessible system. The new tax code must make every effort to benefit the working and middle classes most of all by including tax credits and government rebates for things like renewable energy purchases (solar panels, electric cars) and cost of living deductions. It must also include steep top marginal tax rates for the wealthy and taxes on idle wealth.

90 - Raise Top Marginal Tax Bracket Rates

Most people within the US are financially struggling. Pundits and economic experts say unemployment is down significantly and the stock market is up. Unfortunately this doesn't mean anything to the average American: we don't own stocks and the unemployment rate says nothing about the kinds of employment available, or how much it pays. The reality for average working people is far removed from any good news on Wall Street. And all this while corporations are being subsidized and pay no taxes whatsoever. One thousand, one hundred, or even ten dollars means much more for those living paycheck to paycheck than it does to someone making a year's salary every minute.

It is therefore a requisite that tax rates be overhauled where considerably more Americans pay less if any and considerably few pay considerably more. This will alleviate some of the economic stress on the lower and middle classes. The most economically prosperous times in our country have been when the top marginal tax rates ebbed between 70% and 90% during the 50's through to the 80's. Given the modern astronomical amounts of money garnered by corporations and their CEO's we need to tax every dollar above earned over 10 million at 70% and every dollar over 100 million at 95%. The increased tax revenue can fund various government programs and domestic projects while the average worker will have more in their paychecks.

92 -Tax Wealth And Assets

The divide between the extremely wealthy and the rest of us consists not only of income inequality but massive wealth inequality as well. Multimillionaires and billionaires are able to purchase large assets and make investments that both generate and concentrate more wealth in the hands of a very small number of individuals.

Taxing idle wealth and assets is a necessity to fight obscene inequality. Implementing a 10%, or higher, tax on accumulated wealth over ten million dollars would likely add hundreds of millions if not billions of dollars in revenue annually and we can put some of that idle wealth to work for the general population.

93 - Tax Churches

Churches and religious organizations are actively

pushing policies that give believers of a certain faith special treatment and disingenuously arguing it's a freedom of speech issue. Law makers then create legislation not only guided by their religious beliefs, but are meant to codify them into secular law. Churches of varying sects hold sermons indistinguishable from political rallies and receive billions of dollars in donations every year. Furthermore, few churches actually use those donations to better their neighborhoods or help the less fortunate instead opting for raises and opulent purchases.

Therefore, churches should be taxed like any other business and the money raised could actually go towards good works. The principle of separation between church and state is meant to go both ways whereas what we have now are religious institutions influencing politics and making billions of tax-exempt profit while the state looks the other way. While all religious institutions will be made to pay taxes they would not all pay the same. A megachurch and small country parish feel a flat percentage differently and would thus be taxed along scaling rates. If an individual institution can prove most of its collections are spent on charity they may file for an exempt status or lower rate each year.

94 - End Corporate Welfare

Multibillion dollar corporations across varied industries are paying next to, or literally, nothing in taxes while receiving generous subsidies and even tax refunds. This is corporate welfare and its entire purpose is to make rich people richer while regular people continue struggling and are shamed for taking government assistance.

Companies can no longer be given financial advantages when they are already excessively profitable and worse still serve no purpose benefitting the general public. We must demand of Congress and of our states that they prohibit the practice with legislation and immediately stop supporting a welfare system for multinational billion dollar companies. Subsidies have their place, but they must be limited, temporary and most importantly they must not seek to benefit the bottom line of a company and instead aim to benefit consumers allowing them to make necessary purchases without increasing their cost of living. This can be done without giving corporations tax refunds after paying no income tax and it can be done without even giving corporations themselves backing: vouchers for individuals to use with a company within a specific industry for example would allow the public to choose who is worthy of their business.

95 - Arrest Those Responsible For The 2008 Financial Crisis

Irresponsible, predatory business methods are responsible for creating the 2008 economic crisis and subsequent Great Recession. Certain businesses and the individuals running them made record profits by leaving millions of people to lose their jobs, their homes; forcing hundreds of millions of working Americans to deal with the fallout alongside flat-line wages and rising expenses.

The argument and case is clear for placing responsibility on these bankers and business executives and should be at least delivered to a grand jury. A number of European countries have arrested some these people. The United States should do the same and let a court decide their guilt.

96 - Regulate Finance Industries

Wall Street firms and big banks are responsible for the massive economic crisis in 2008 and continue to reap the benefits of irresponsible and predatory business practices. Approving people who will likely default for loans and even overdraft and ATM fees are just a few of the ways companies in the finance industry take advantage of ordinary people in pursuit of their next bonus. The finance sector is complicated and its inner workings are far removed from the daily lives of ordinary people. This makes it difficult for individuals to fight back against them and keeps the public disinterested while these industries write their own regulations.

We can no longer allow this industry as a whole continue setting people up to fail and then preying upon them when they do. Private banks can no longer continue making money with our money and leaving us with nothing to show for it. We require new regulations that are written by consumers and with their welfare in mind and not corporate interests.

97 - End Debt Trading

Debt buying in the United States is a predatory industry where freelance debt collectors intimidate people into paying more than can afford and sometimes try to collect debts that have already been resolved. People within the industry wrote the regulations, giving themselves every advantage and benefit of the doubt over debtors.

Debt buying, or debt trading, is the practice of buying and selling ownership over a debt. Banks, businesses, and private individuals buy a debt from another party, usually for cents on the dollar. So whoever had to pay the debt will now be paying it to a separate third party not involved in any way during the original transaction responsible for incurring the debt. The original party sells when they believe the debtor will be unlikely to pay back the debt and they'd rather have a smaller guaranteed sum in the present and forfeit the risk. The party buying the debt then assumes risk of non-payment, but stand to make an incredible amount of profit given what they paid for it. The problems arise from a number of regulatory oversights: the accessibility to licensure to become a debt buyer allows almost anyone to legally do this; there's no real protections for consumers against unethical collection methods; the records can be bought and sold so often that they're no longer up to date, or even valid because of statutes of limitation, but the way current laws are written the new owners of a debt that's no longer valid, or has even been paid, can still try to collect it - sometimes referred to as "zombie debt."

Being the target of a debt collector is stressful enough without the addition of harassment from difficult to regulate, difficult to track third parties. It's inconvenient at best and life ruing at worst. Protections against debt collectors for consumers written by consumers should be enacted into law alongside more scrutiny on those collecting debts. However, the actual trading of debt itself cannot be properly regulated and third parties have no purpose in business dealings between two others without the consent of both parties involved and so must be abolished.

98 - End "Too Big To Fail"

The argument supporting the 2008 bailout for failed businesses predicted the financial fallout from letting these businesses fail would be worse than what they already did to the economy. The financial institutions responsible for crashing the world economy were saved and the millions of Americans left struggling simply written off as a necessary sacrifice: people lost their homes and life savings while criminals in finance received bonuses. And yet, because of their size, the number of homes, jobs, 401ks, and lives in general built upon the tendrils of these fragile giants had those giants fell the cascading consequences would have been felt even further through our society.

If a financial entity can be large enough to impact the world economy so significantly it should not exist. Financial giants must be broken up into smaller entities by enforcing existing anti-trust laws and instituting a stricter code of ethics on their business practices. The tentacles of cancerous titans of industry must be severed because too big to fail is too big to exist.

99 - Place Needs Above Profits

Every single day people are dying because they can't afford their prescriptions; regular checkups; ambulance rides. People are dying because they can't afford to eat well enough if at all; they can't afford to avoid drinking lead and toxin tainted water; and dying of exposure because they cannot pay for shelter. These are basic and fundamental human needs and requiring payment for them literally holds people hostage to their bank accounts and their jobs. Capitalism and the free market have not created a dramatic reduction in price with simultaneous increases in quality that free market competition promised by capitalism.

It is therefore necessary to abolish selling necessities for profit. We require legislation and a Constitutional amendment prohibiting for-profit sales of water and medicine along with strict limitations on non-prepared foods. The bottom line for industries supplying human necessities will no longer be their profit margins; it will instead be saving lives and bettering the quality of those lives. We already produce more than we consume, we only need to disperse our resources properly.

Bibliographies

Education

"Alternative Education." *K12 Academics*, K12 Academics, 6 Feb. 2014, www.k12academics.com/alternative-education.

Bridges, Emily, and Debra Hauser. "Youth Health and Rights in Sex Education." *Future of Sex Ed*, Advocates for Youth, May 2014, www.futureofsexed.org/youthhealthrights.html.

Benavides, Lucia, and Sebastian Vega. "Tired of 'Whitewashed' Curriculum, Black Texans Turn to Homeschooling." *Texas Standard*, 9 July 2015, www.texasstandard.org/stories/texas-schools-curriculum-whitewash-african-american-history/.

Dillard, Coshandra. "Five Ways to Avoid Whitewashing the Civil Rights Movement." *Teaching Tolerance*, 1 Jan. 2019, www.tolerance.org/magazine/five-ways-to-avoid-whitewashing-the-civil-rights-movement.

Ford, James E. "We Need to Start Telling the Truth About White Supremacy in Our Schools." *Education Post*, 13 Dec. 2016, educationpost.org/we-need-to-start-telling-the-truth-about-white-supremacy-in-our-schools/.

Harriot, Michael. "Millions of Students Are Quietly Being Taught the Koch Brothers' Whitewashed Version of Black History." *The Root*, The Root, 14 Mar. 2018, www.theroot.com/millions-of-students-are-quietly-being-taught-the-koch-1823742091.

Lynch, Matthew. "Poverty and School Funding: Why Low-Income Students Often Suffer." *The Edvocate*, 6 Feb. 2016, www.theedadvocate.org/poverty-and-school-funding-why-low-income-students-often-suffer/.

Miller, Ron. "A Map of the Alternative Education Landscape." *AERO (Alternative Education Resource*

Organization),
www.educationrevolution.org/store/resources/alternatives/
mapoflandscape/.
Originally published in *Paths of Learning* #20 (Spring, 2004).

Noack, Rick. "Why Danish Students Are Paid to Go to
College." *The Washington Post*, WP Company, 4 Feb.
2015,
www.washingtonpost.com/news/worldviews/wp/2015/02/0
4/why-danish-students-are-paid-to-go-to-
college/?noredirect=on&utm_term=.11a13d0c5a3a.

Niose, David. "Anti-Intellectualism Is Killing
America." *Psychology Today*, Sussex Publishers, 23 June
2015, www.psychologytoday.com/us/blog/our-humanity-
naturally/201506/anti-intellectualism-is-killing-america.

Nursing@USC Staff. "America's Sex Education: How We Are
Failing Our Students." *Department of Nursing*, University
of Southern California, 18 Sept. 2017,
nursing.usc.edu/blog/americas-sex-education/.

Reeves, Douglas. "Leading to Change: How Do You Change
School Culture?" *Educational Leadership*, Association for
ASCD (Association for Supervision and Curriculum
Development), www.ascd.org/publications/educational-
leadership/dec06/vol64/num04/How-Do-You-Change-
School-Culture¢.aspx.
Originally published *Science in the Spotlight*. Volume 64,
Number 4, Pages 92-94. December 2006/January 2007

Rosenberg, Paul. "America's Growing Anti-Intellectualism."*Al
Jazeera, US & Canada*, Al Jazeera, 12 Oct. 2011,
www.aljazeera.com/indepth/opinion/2011/10/20111091127
27162598.html.

Turner, Cory. "America's Schools Are 'Profoundly Unequal,'
Says U.S. Civil Rights Commission." *NPR*, NPR, 11 Jan.
2018,
www.npr.org/sections/ed/2018/01/11/577000301/americas-

schools-are-profoundly-unequal-says-u-s-civil-rights-commission.

Sherman, Zander. "Students Should Be Paid to Study." *HuffPost*, HuffPost, 13 Jan. 2018, www.huffpost.com/entry/students-should-be-paid-to-study_b_5a5a4121e4b003efadb6ae35.

"Why Comprehensive Sexuality Education Is Important." *UNESCO*, 15 Feb. 2018, en.unesco.org/news/why-comprehensive-sexuality-education-important.

Media And Technology

Ford, Anne. "The Surprising Speed with Which We Become Polarized Online." *Kellogg Insight*, Kellogg School of Managment at Northwestern Univeristy, 6 Apr. 2017, insight.kellogg.northwestern.edu/article/the-surprising-speed-with-which-we-become-polarized-online.

Hao, Karen. "DeepMind Is Asking How AI Helped Turn the Internet into an Echo Chamber." *MIT Technology Review*, MIT Technology Review, 8 Mar. 2019, www.technologyreview.com/s/613083/deepmind-is-asking-how-google-helped-turn-the-internet-into-an-echo-chamber/.

Mason, Lance E, et al. "Media Literacy, Democracy, and the Challenge of Fake News." *Journal of Media Literacy Education* , 2 Nov. 2018. digitalcommons.uri.edu/.

Saldana, Dave. "A Law Against Lying on the News." *YES! Magazine*, 17 Mar. 2011, www.yesmagazine.org/people-power/a-law-against-lying-on-the-news.

Sardo, Bianca Christine, et al. "The Environmental Consequences in a Process of Planned Obsolescence of Mobile Phones." *AJER (American Journal of Engineering Research)*, vol. 7, no. 5, 21 May 2018, pp. 389–396. ajer.org.

"Tell Apple, Samsung and LG to Design Repairable, Long-Lasting Products!" *Rethink-It*, www.rethink-it.org/.

Trammel, Travis. "A Structure to Counter Fake News." *Stanford PACS*, 8 Jan. 2018, pacscenter.stanford.edu/.

Energy

Aronoff, Kate. "Fossil Fuels Are a Threat to Civilization, New U.N. Report Concludes." *The Intercept*, 9 Oct. 2018, theintercept.com/2018/10/09/un-report-climate-change-fossil-fuels/.

Conca, James. "It's Final -- Corn Ethanol Is Of No Use." *Forbes*, Forbes Magazine, 26 Apr. 2014, www.forbes.com/sites/jamesconca/2014/04/20/its-final-corn-ethanol-is-of-no-use/#1c689cf667d3.

DeGood, Kevin, et al. "Building Progressive Infrastructure." *Center for American Progress*, 31 Jan. 2019, www.americanprogress.org/issues/economy/reports/2019/01/31/465687/building-progressive-infrastructure/.

Fischetti, Mark. "How to Power the World without Fossil Fuels." *Scientific American*, 15 Apr. 2013, www.scientificamerican.com/article/how-to-power-the-world/?redirect=1.

Leonard, Annie. "If We Don't Stop Producing Fossil Fuels, We Won't Make It." *Greenpeace USA*, 10 Jan. 2019, www.greenpeace.org/usa/if-we-dont-stop-producing-fossil-fuels-we-wont-make-it/.

Runge, C. Ford. "The Case Against More Ethanol: It's Simply Bad for Environment." *Yale Environment 360*, Yale School of Forestry & Environmental Studies, 25 May 2016, e360.yale.edu/features/the_case_against_ethanol_bad_for_environment.

Sadasivam, Naveena. "Fracking Studies Overwhelmingly Indicate Threats to Public Health." *InsideClimate News*, 3 Jan. 2017, insideclimatenews.org/news/16102015/fracking-studies-overwhelmingly-indicate-threats-public-health-air-water-pollution.

Schrope, Mark. "Fracking Outpaces Science on Its Impact." *Yale FES Website*, Yale School of Forestry and Environmental Studies, environment.yale.edu/envy/stories/fracking-outpaces-science-on-its-impact#gsc.tab=0.

Stewart, Jack. "America Gets a D Plus for Infrastructure, and a Big Bill to Fix It." *Wired*, Conde Nast, 3 Sept. 2017, www.wired.com/2017/03/america-gets-d-plus-infrastructure-big-bill-fix/.

Vaidyanathan, Gayathri. "Fracking Can Contaminate Drinking Water." *Scientific American*, 4 Apr. 2016, www.scientificamerican.com/article/fracking-can-contaminate-drinking-water/.
Reprinted in Scientific American from Climatewire with permission from Environment & Energy Publishing, LLC.

"What Is a Green New Deal?" *Sierra Club*, 27 Nov. 2018, www.sierraclub.org/trade/what-green-new-deal.

Food and Nutrition

Carney, Megan. "Making Healthy School Lunches Free for All Should Be a National Priority." *Civil Eats*, 14 Dec. 2018, civileats.com/2018/12/14/making-healthy-school-lunches-free-for-all-should-be-a-national-priority/.

Daschle, Tom, and Richard B Myers. "A Threat to the Food System." *U.S. News & World Report*, U.S. News & World Report, 17 Oct. 2016, www.usnews.com/opinion/articles/2016-10-17/americas-food-supply-and-national-security-are-at-risk-to-bioterrorism.

"Food Security and the Right to Food." *Food and Agriculture Organization of the United Nations*, www.fao.org/sustainable-development-goals/overview/fao-and-the-post-2015-development-agenda/food-security-and-the-right-to-food/en/.

Haspel, Tamar. "Monocrops: They're a Problem, but Farmers Aren't the Ones Who Can Solve It." *The Washington Post*, WP Company, 9 May 2014, www.washingtonpost.com/lifestyle/food/monocrops-theyre-a-problem-but-farmers-arent-the-ones-who-can-solve-it/2014/05/09/8bfc186e-d6f8-11e3-8a78-8fe50322a72c_story.html?utm_term=.02b107533490.

"It's Time to Ban Factory Farms." *Food & Water Watch*, 14 May 2018, www.foodandwaterwatch.org/news/its-time-ban-factory-farms.

Kenner, Robert, director. *Food Inc. POV*, Public Broadcasting Service (PBS).

Levin, Madeleine, and Jessie Hewins. "Universal Free School Meals." *Clearinghouse Community*, Sargent Shriver National Center on Poverty Law, 2014, www.povertylaw.org/clearinghouse/articles/meals.

Levine, James A. *Poverty and Obesity in the U.S.* American Diabetes Association, 1 Nov. 2011, diabetes.diabetesjournals.org/content/60/11/2667.

Stewart, Emily. "America's Monopoly Problem, in One Chart." *Vox*, Vox, 26 Nov. 2018, www.vox.com/2018/11/26/18112651/monopoly-open-markets-institute-report-concentration.

"The Economic Cost of Food Monopolies." *Food & Water Watch*, 2 Nov. 2012, www.foodandwaterwatch.org/insight/economic-cost-food-monopolies.

Zee, Bibi van der. "Why Factory Farming Is Not Just Cruel – but Also a Threat to All Life on the Planet." *The Guardian*, Guardian News and Media, 4 Oct. 2017, www.theguardian.com/environment/2017/oct/04/factory-farming-destructive-wasteful-cruel-says-philip-lymbery-farmageddon-author.

Medical

"A Legislative Guide to Advocating for Stronger Vaccine Laws." *VAXOPEDIA*, 22 Feb. 2019, vaxopedia.org/2019/02/21/a-legislative-guide-to-advocating-for-stronger-vaccine-laws/.

Brown, Dana. "Before Big Pharma Kills Us, Maybe Public Pharma Can Save Us." *The American Prospect*, 27 Aug. 2018, prospect.org/article/big-pharma-kills-us-maybe-public-pharma-can-save-us.

Cohen, Pieter, et al. "Is ADHD Overdiagnosed and Overtreated?" *Harvard Health Publishing*, Harvard Medical School, 18 Mar. 2017, www.health.harvard.edu/blog/is-adhd-overdiagnosed-and-overtreated-2017031611304.

Frances, Allen J. "Pharma Corruption Started the Opioid Epidemic." *Psychology Today*, Sussex Publishers, 4 Oct. 2017, www.psychologytoday.com/us/blog/saving-normal/201710/pharma-corruption-started-the-opioid-epidemic.

Knickman, James, et al. "Improving Access to Effective Care for People Who Have Mental Health and Substance Use Disorders." *The National Academy of Medicine's Vital Directions for Health and Health Care*, California Health Care Foundation, The Commonwealth Fund, the Gordon and Betty Moore Foundation, The John A. Hartford Foundation, the Josiah Macy Jr. Foundation, the Robert Wood Johnson Foundation, and the National Academy of Medicine's Harvey V. Fineberg Impact Fund., 19 Sept. 2016, nam.edu/wp-content/uploads/2016/09/Improving-

Access-to-Effective-Care-for-People-Who-Have-Mental-Health-and-Sustance-Use-Disorders.pdf.

Lane, Christopher. "ADHD Is Now Widely Overdiagnosed and for Multiple Reasons." *Psychology Today*, Sussex Publishers, 20 Oct. 2017, www.psychologytoday.com/us/blog/side-effects/201710/adhd-is-now-widely-overdiagnosed-and-multiple-reasons.

Lieberman, Jeffrey, et al. *Improving Mental Health Care in America: An Opportunity for Comprehensive Reform.* Psychiatric Times. Available at: https://www.psychiatrictimes.com/cultural-psychiatry/improving-mental-health-care-america-opportunity-comprehensive-reform

Lurie, Julia. "'Behave More Sexually:" How Big Pharma Used Strippers, Guns, and Cash to Push Opioids." *Mother Jones*, 1 Feb. 2019, www.motherjones.com/politics/2018/05/insys-subsys-whistleblower-lawsuits/.

Mukhopadhyay, Tanni. "Women's Reproductive Rights Are Human Rights." *Human Development Reports*, United Nations Development Program, 11 July 2017, hdr.undp.org/en/content/women's-reproductive-rights-are-human-rights.

Sen, Amartya, and Thomas W Lamont. "Universal Health Care: The Affordable Dream." *Harvard Public Health Review*, Harvard Public Health Review, 2015, harvardpublichealthreview.org/universal-health-care-the-affordable-dream/.

"UN Human Rights Committee Asserts That Access to Abortion and Prevention of Maternal Mortality Are Human Rights." *Center for Reproductive Rights*, 31 Oct. 2018, www.reproductiverights.org/press-room/un-committee-asserts-that-access-to-abortion-and-prevention-of-maternal-death-are-human-rights.

"Universal Access to Contraception, Policy Number: 20153." *American Public Health Association*, 3 Nov. 2015, www.apha.org/policies-and-advocacy/public-health-policy-statements/policy-database/2015/12/17/09/14/universal-access-to-contraception.

Civil Rights

Barajas, Joshua. "Police Deploy Water Hoses, Tear Gas against Standing Rock Protesters." *PBS*, Public Broadcasting Service, 21 Nov. 2016, www.pbs.org/newshour/nation/police-deploy-water-hoses-tear-gas-against-standing-rock-protesters.

Brustin, Stacy. "I Toured an Immigration Detention Center. The Prison-like Atmosphere Was Mind-Numbing." *USA Today*, Gannett Satellite Information Network, 16 May 2019, www.usatoday.com/story/opinion/voices/2019/05/16/ice-immigration-detention-center-like-prison-otero-column/1190633001/.

Bullock, Scott, and Dana Berliner. "Eminent Domain Abuse Hurts America: Column." *USA Today*, Gannett Satellite Information Network, 23 Feb. 2015, www.usatoday.com/story/opinion/2015/02/23/kelo-supreme-court-city-homes-development-column/23673563/.

Coaston, Jane. "Eminent Domain, the Big-Government Tactic Trump Needs to Use to Build the Wall, Explained." *Vox*, Vox, 18 Jan. 2019, www.vox.com/policy-and-politics/2019/1/18/18176893/eminent-domain-trump-border-wall-gop.

DeSilver, Drew. "Weekday Elections Set the U.S. Apart from Many Other Advanced Democracies." *Pew Research Center*, Pew Research Center, 6 Nov. 2018, www.pewresearch.org/fact-tank/2018/11/06/weekday-elections-set-the-u-s-apart-from-many-other-advanced-democracies/.

"Evidence of Global Opposition to US Mass Surveillance." *Mass Surveillance* , Amnesty International UK, www.amnesty.org.uk/mass-surveillance-us-nsa-edward-snowden-gchq.

Franke-Ruta, Garance. "Too Much Violence and Pepper Spray at the OWS Protests: The Videos and Pictures." *The Atlantic*, Atlantic Media Company, 19 Nov. 2011, www.theatlantic.com/politics/archive/2011/11/too-much-violence-and-pepper-spray-at-the-ows-protests-the-videos-and-pictures/248761/.

Gallagher, Ryan, and Henrik Moltke. "The NSA's Hidden Spy Hubs in Eight U.S. Cities." *The Intercept*, 25 June 2018, theintercept.com/2018/06/25/att-internet-nsa-spy-hubs/.

Gary, Juneau, PsyD and Neal S. Rubin PhD. *"Are LGBT rights human rights? Recent developments at the United Nations."* American Psychological Association , 2 June. 2012, https://www.apa.org/international/pi/2012/06/un-matters

Gellman, Barton, and Sam Adler-Bell. "The Disparate Impact of Surveillance." *The Century Foundation*, 21 Dec. 2017, tcf.org/content/report/disparate-impact-surveillance/?session=1.

Graf, Nikki, et al. "The Narrowing, but Persistent, Gender Gap in Pay." *Pew Research Center*, Pew Research Center, 22 Mar. 2019, www.pewresearch.org/fact-tank/2019/03/22/gender-pay-gap-facts/.

Hegewisch, Ariane, et al. "The Gender Wage Gap: 2018 Earnings Differences by Race and Ethnicity." *Institute for Women's Policy Research*, 7 Mar. 2019, iwpr.org/publications/gender-wage-gap-2018/.

Kim, Jennifer. "'Public Needs' Abuse Eminent Domain for Economic Development." *Brown Political Review*, 29 Oct.

2015, www.brownpoliticalreview.org/2015/10/public-needs-abuse-eminent-domain-for-economic-development/.

Kirby, Jen. "Nearly 600 Women Arrested at Immigration Protests in Senate Building." *Vox*, Vox, 29 June 2018, www.vox.com/2018/6/28/17515160/womens-march-protests-family-separation-600-arrested.

Lines, Fault. "The Dark Prisoners: Inside the CIA's Torture Programme." *Al Jazeera USA*, Al Jazeera, 14 Sept. 2016, www.aljazeera.com/indepth/features/2016/03/dark-prisoners-cia-torture-programme-160326051331796.html.

Lopez, German. "Trump Promised to Be LGBTQ-Friendly. His First Year in Office Proved It Was a Giant Con." *Vox*, Vox, 22 Jan. 2018, www.vox.com/identities/2018/1/22/16905658/trump-lgbtq-anniversary.

Martin, Areva. "Weight Discrimination Is Legal in 49 States." *Time*, Time, 16 Aug. 2017, time.com/4883176/weight-discrimination-workplace-laws/.

McDonald, Annie. "Ensuring Access to Election Day for All." *Berkeley Public Policy Journal*, 6 Nov. 2018, bppj.berkeley.edu/2018/11/06/ensuring-access-to-election-day-for-all/.

Medina, Daniel A. and Chiara A. Sottlie. "Dozens Arrested as Thousands Take Dakota Pipeline Protest National." *NBC News*, Universal News Group, 16 Nov. 2016, www.nbcnews.com/storyline/dakota-pipeline-protests/scores-arrested-dakota-access-pipeline-protests-nationwide-n684531.

Michael, Maggie. "The US Is Still Helping to Run 'Black Site' Prisons Where Detainees Are Allegedly Abused and Tortured." *Business Insider*, Business Insider, 22 June 2017, www.businessinsider.com/the-us-is-still-helping-run-black-site-prisons-where-detainees-allegedly-abused-tortured-2017-6.

Miles, Tom. "U.N. Expert Says Torture Persists at Guantanamo Bay; U.S. Denies." *Reuters*, Thomson Reuters, 13 Dec. 2017, www.reuters.com/article/us-usa-guantanamo-torture/u-n-expert-says-torture-persists-at-guantanamo-bay-u-s-denies-idUSKBN1E71QO.

"More than 80 Arrested during Sacramento Police Shooting Protest." *USA News Al Jazeera*, Al Jazeera, 5 Mar. 2019, www.aljazeera.com/news/2019/03/80-arrested-sacramento-police-shooting-protest-190305190729194.html.

Ngabirano, Anne-Marcelle. "'Pink Tax' Forces Women to Pay More than Men." *USA Today*, Gannett Satellite Information Network, 27 Mar. 2017, www.usatoday.com/story/money/business/2017/03/27/pink-tax-forces-women-pay-more-than-men/99462846/.

Ortiz, Jorge L. "Tear Gas: 'Harsh, Terrifying' and Legal to Use on Civilians (and Immigrants)." *USA Today*, Gannett Satellite Information Network, 27 Nov. 2018, www.usatoday.com/story/news/2018/11/27/tear-gas-forbidden-war-but-legal-use-civilians-and-migrants/2133144002/.

Powell, Tia, et al. "Transgender Rights as Human Rights." *AMA Journal of Ethics*, vol. 18, no. 11, Nov. 2016, pp. 1126–1131., journalofethics.ama-assn.org/sites/journalofethics.ama-assn.org/files/2018-05/pfor3-1611.pdf.

"Surveillance Under the Patriot Act." *American Civil Liberties Union*, ACLU, 2019, www.aclu.org/issues/national-security/privacy-and-surveillance/surveillance-under-patriot-act.

Shetty, Salil. "Solving the 'Big Brother Problem' of Mass Surveillance." *Amnesty International USA*, 23 Jan. 2014, www.amnestyusa.org/solving-the-big-brother-problem-of-mass-surveillance/.

Singh, Amrit. "Europe's Human Rights Court Shines More
    Light on the CIA's Black Site Torture Program." *Open
    Society Foundations*, 8 June 2018,
    www.opensocietyfoundations.org/voices/europe-s-human-
    rights-court-shines-more-light-cia-s-black-site-torture-
    program.

Stanglin, Doug, and Herb Jackson. "'Kava Nope': Police Arrest
    164 as Anti-Kavanaugh Protesters Take to Capitol
    Steps." *USA Today*, Gannett Satellite Information Network,
    7 Oct. 2018,
    www.usatoday.com/story/news/2018/10/06/police-clear-
    capitol-steps-chanting-protesters-ahead-kavanaugh-
    vote/1548499002/.

*"The Lies and Dangers of Efforts to Change Orientation or
    Gender Identity."* Human Rights Campaign, 2019,
    https://www.hrc.org/resources/the-lies-and-dangers-of-
    reparative-therapy

Tong, Traci. "U.S. Coast Guard Operating Secret Floating
    Prisons in Pacific Ocean." *USA Today*, Gannett Satellite
    Information Network, 28 Nov. 2017,
    www.usatoday.com/story/news/world/2017/11/28/u-s-
    coast-guard-operating-secret-floating-prisons-pacific-
    ocean/900462001/.

"United States: State Laws Threaten LGBT Equality." *Human
    Rights Watch*, 19 Feb. 2018,
    www.hrw.org/news/2018/02/19/united-states-state-laws-
    threaten-lgbt-equality#.

Vasquez, Tina. "'People Were Gasping and Terrified': Excessive
    Police Force in Phoenix After Trump's Rally
    Tuesday." *Rewire.News*, Rewire.News, 25 Aug. 2017,
    rewire.news/article/2017/08/25/people-gasping-terrified-
    excessive-police-force-phoenix-trumps-rally-tuesday/.

Wakeman, Jessica. *"The Real Cost of the Pink Tax."* Healthline,
    2 Aug. 2018, https://www.healthline.com/health/the-real-
    cost-of-pink-tax#17

Law Enforcement

Abdul, Geneva. "It's Legal to Sell Sex in Amsterdam, But Don't Expect the Same Rights As Other Workers." *Foreign Policy*, Foreign Policy, 19 Feb. 2019, foreignpolicy.com/2019/02/19/its-legal-to-sell-sex-in-amsterdam-but-dont-expect-the-same-rights-as-other-self-employed-workers-netherlands-legal-prostitution-sex-workers/.

Beitsch, Rebecca. "Tiny Houses Are Trendy, Minimalist and Often Illegal." *PBS*, Public Broadcasting Service, 6 July 2016, www.pbs.org/newshour/nation/tiny-houses-are-trendy-minimalist-and-often-illegal.

Fleiss, Heidi. "Hollywood Madam: Want to Stop Human Trafficking? Legalize Consensual Sex for Money." *USA Today*, Gannett Satellite Information Network, 27 Feb. 2019, www.usatoday.com/story/opinion/voices/2019/02/27/robert-kraft-affidavit-details-threesome-sandwich-indictment-police-report-column/2982383002/.

Gunderson, Anne. "The Effect of Decriminalizing Prostitution on Public Health and Safety." *Chicago Policy Review*, 26 Feb. 2018, chicagopolicyreview.org/2018/02/26/the-effect-of-decriminalizing-prostitution-on-public-health-and-safety/.

"Lethal Injection." *Last Week Tonight with John Oliver*, HBO, 5 may. 2019.

Segura, Liliana. "Ohio's Governor Stopped an Execution Over Fears It Would Feel Like Waterboarding." *The Intercept*, The Intercept, 7 Feb. 2019, theintercept.com/2019/02/07/death-penalty-lethal-injection-midazolam-ohio/.

Subbaraman, Nidhi, and Chris McDaniel. "A Man On Death Row Is Fighting To Die By Electrocution. These Documents Show The Horrifying History Of The Chair

That Would Be Used." *BuzzFeed News*, BuzzFeed, 12 Oct. 2018, www.buzzfeednews.com/article/nidhisubbaraman/electric-chair-tennessee-edmund-zagorski.

"True Story: I'm A Sex Worker." *Yes and Yes*, 10 Oct. 2011, yesandyes.org/2011/10/true-story-im-sex-worker.html.

Tsoulis-Reay, Alexa. "What It's Like to Be a Legal Sex Worker in New Zealand." *The Cut*, The Cut, 8 Mar. 2018, www.thecut.com/2018/03/what-its-like-to-be-a-legal-sex-worker-in-new-zealand.html.
By Bubbles as told to Alexa Tsoulis-Reay

Government

Alexander, David. "Pentagon Buried Study That Found $125 Billion in Wasteful Spending:..." *Reuters*, Thomson Reuters, 6 Dec. 2016, www.reuters.com/article/us-usa-defense-waste/pentagon-buried-study-that-found-125-billion-in-wasteful-spending-washington-post-idUSKBN13V08B.

"Alternative Voting Systems."*National Conference of State Legislatures*, National Conference of State Legislatures, 20 Oct. 2017, www.ncsl.org/research/elections-and-campaigns/alternative-voting-systems.aspx.

Amar, Akhil Reed. "Election 2016: The Real Reason the Electoral College Exists." *Time*, Time, 8 Nov. 2016, time.com/4558510/electoral-college-history-slavery/.

"Arguments for Nuclear Abolition." *The International Campaign to Abolish Nuclear Weapons*, The International Campaign to Abolish Nuclear Weapons, 2019, www.icanw.org/why-a-ban/arguments-for-a-ban/.

Badger, Emily. "As American as Apple Pie? The Rural Vote's Disproportionate Slice of Power." *The New York Times*, The New York Times, 20 Nov. 2016, www.nytimes.com/2016/11/21/upshot/as-american-as-apple-pie-the-rural-votes-disproportionate-slice-of-power.html.

Berman, Russell. "An Exodus From Congress Tests the Lure of Lobbying." *The Atlantic*, Atlantic Media Company, 1 May 2018, www.theatlantic.com/politics/archive/2018/05/lobbying-the-job-of-choice-for-retired-members-of-congress/558851/.

Bokhari, Adnan, and Ola Wadibia. "Removing Financial Barriers for Immigrants Is a Boon to America's Overall Prosperity." *Prosperity Now*, Prosperity Now, 16 Aug. 2018, prosperitynow.org/blog/removing-financial-barriers-immigrants-boon-americas-overall-prosperity.

Burgat, Casey. "The House Asked Members for Their Ideas to Make Congress Work Better. This Is What They Suggested." *Brookings*, Brookings Institute, 21 Sept. 2018, www.brookings.edu/blog/fixgov/2018/09/21/the-house-asked-members-for-their-ideas-to-make-congress-work-better-this-is-what-they-suggested/.

Chappell, Bill. "U.S. Strips Visa From World Criminal Court Prosecutor Pursuing War-Crimes Inquiry." *NPR*, NPR, 5 Apr. 2019, www.npr.org/2019/04/05/710324238/u-s-strips-visa-from-intl-criminal-court-prosecutor-pursuing-war-crime-inquiry.

Cheng, Amrit. "3 Reasons Why Immigration Detention Centers Are Not Like 'Summer Camp'." *American Civil Liberties Union*, American Civil Liberties Union, 2 Aug. 2018, www.aclu.org/blog/immigrants-rights/immigrants-rights-and-detention/3-reasons-why-immigration-detention-centers.

Cowen, Tyler. "The Aliens Among Us." *Bloomberg*, Bloomberg, 1 May 2019, www.bloomberg.com/opinion/articles/2019-05-02/ufo-sightings-u-s-military-takes-them-seriously-you-should-too.

Drake, Nadia. "What Weve Learned From 60 Years of U.S.-Funded UFO Probes." *National Geographic*, National Geographic Society, 19 Dec. 2017, news.nationalgeographic.com/2017/12/pentagon-ufos-search-extraterrestrial-intelligence-life-space-science/.

Dunlop, Tim. "Voting Undermines the Will of the People – It's Time to Replace It with Sortition." *The Guardian*, Guardian News and Media, 13 Oct. 2018, www.theguardian.com/australia-news/2018/oct/14/voting-undermines-the-will-of-the-people-its-time-to-replace-it-with-sortition.
This is an edited extract from Tim Dunlop's The Future of Everything: Big, audacious ideas for a better world.

"Elected Judges." *Last Week Tonight with John Oliver*, HBO, 23 Feb. 2015.

"Fact Sheet: Why Don't They Just Get In Line?" *American Immigration Council*, American Immigration Council, 12 Aug. 2016, www.americanimmigrationcouncil.org/research/why-don't-they-just-get-line.

Fernandez, Belen. "Under Fire: the Perpetual US War on Native Americans." *USA | Al Jazeera*, Al Jazeera, 9 Aug. 2018, www.aljazeera.com/indepth/opinion/fire-perpetual-war-native-americans-180809091526835.html.

"Frequently Asked Questions." *Native American Rights Fund*, Native American Rights Fund, www.narf.org/frequently-asked-questions/.

Hacker, Jason S, and Nathan Loewentheil. "How Big Money Corrupts the Economy." *Democracy Journal*, Democracy: A Journal of Ideas, Inc., 2013, democracyjournal.org/magazine/27/how-big-money-corrupts-the-economy/.

Hallman, Hunter. "How Do Undocumented Immigrants Pay Federal Taxes? An Explainer." *Bipartisan Policy Center*, 28 Mar. 2018, bipartisanpolicy.org/blog/how-do-undocumented-immigrants-pay-federal-taxes-an-explainer/.

Hansen, Claire. "116th Congress by Party, Race, Gender, and Religion." *U.S. News & World Report*, U.S. News & World Report, 3 Jan. 2019, www.usnews.com/news/politics/slideshows/116th-congress-by-party-race-gender-and-religion?onepage.

Hawkings, David. "Wealth of Congress: Richer Than Ever, but Mostly at the Very Top." *Roll Call*, Roll Call, 27 Feb. 2018, www.rollcall.com/news/hawkings/congress-richer-ever-mostly-top.

Hussain, Murtaza. "The U.S. Goes to War Against the ICC to Cover Up Alleged War Crimes in Afghanistan." *The Intercept*, The Intercept, 12 Sept. 2018, theintercept.com/2018/09/12/john-bolton-icc-afghanistan-war-crimes/.

John, Paige St., and Joel Rubin. "ICE Held an American Man in Custody for 1,273 Days. He's Not the Only One Who Had to Prove His Citizenship." *Los Angeles Times*, Los Angeles Times, 17 Sept. 2018, www.latimes.com/local/lanow/la-me-citizens-ice-20180427-htmlstory.html.

Jones, Bradley. "Most Americans Want to Limit Campaign Spending." *Pew Research Center*, Pew Research Center, 8 May 2018, www.pewresearch.org/fact-tank/2018/05/08/most-americans-want-to-limit-campaign-spending-say-big-donors-have-greater-political-influence/.

Koger, Gregory. "How to Fix Congress: Start with the Basics." *Vox*, Vox, 28 Nov. 2017, www.vox.com/mischiefs-of-faction/2017/11/28/16705128/how-to-fix-congress.

Ladd, Jonathan M. "The Senate Is a Much Bigger Problem than the Electoral College." *Vox*, Vox, 9 Apr. 2019,

www.vox.com/mischiefs-of-
faction/2019/4/9/18300749/senate-problem-electoral-
college.

Lapowsky, Issie. "A Dead-Simple Algorithm Reveals the True
    Toll of Voter ID Laws." *Wired*, Conde Nast, 4 Jan. 2018,
    www.wired.com/story/voter-id-law-algorithm/.

Larison, Daniel. "War with Venezuela Is Unnecessary, Illegal,
    and Wrong." *The American Conservative*, The American
    Conservative, 1 May 2019,
    www.theamericanconservative.com/larison/war-with-
    venezuela-is-unnecessary-illegal-and-wrong/.

Lawrence, Kerri. "Do Records Show Proof of UFOs?" *National
    Archives and Records Administration*, National Archives
    and Records Administration, 9 Feb. 2018,
    www.archives.gov/news/articles/do-records-show-proof-of-
    ufos.

Longley, Robert. "What are Rider Bills in Government?"
    ThoughtCo, Dec. 6, 2018, thoughtco.com/rider-bills-in-the-
    us-congress-stealth-legislation-4090449.

Lopez, German. "A New Study Finds Voter ID Laws Don't
    Reduce Voter Fraud - or Voter Turnout." *Vox*, Vox, 21 Feb.
    2019, www.vox.com/policy-and-
    politics/2019/2/21/18230009/voter-id-laws-fraud-turnout-
    study-research.

Lopez, German. "John Oliver Explains Why Elected Judges Are
    Terrible for American Democracy." *Vox*, Vox, 23 Feb.
    2015, www.vox.com/2015/2/23/8090203/john-oliver-
    judicial-elections.

Marchand, Ross. "The F-35, the Great White Whale of Defense
    Waste." *Washington Examiner*, Washington Examiner, 14
    Nov. 2018, www.washingtonexaminer.com/opinion/op-
    eds/the-f-35-the-great-white-whale-of-defense-waste.

McElwee, Sean. "It's Time to Abolish ICE." *The Nation*, The Nation, 9 Mar. 2018, www.thenation.com/article/its-time-to-abolish-ice/.

Newkirk II, Vann R. "Voter Suppression Is Warping Democracy." *The Atlantic*, Atlantic Media Company, 17 July 2018, www.theatlantic.com/politics/archive/2018/07/poll-prri-voter-suppression/565355/.

O'Neel, Danny. "I Survived Combat in Iraq and a Suicide Attempt at Home. But Many Veterans Aren't so Lucky." *USA Today*, Gannett Satellite Information Network, 16 Jan. 2019, www.usatoday.com/story/opinion/voices/2019/01/16/vetera n-affairs-suicide-military-iraq-war-column/2580957002/.

"Oppose Voter ID Legislation - Fact Sheet." *American Civil Liberties Union*, American Civil Liberties Union, 2019, www.aclu.org/other/oppose-voter-id-legislation-fact-sheet.

"Pakistani Civilians." *Pakistani Civilians | Costs of War*, Brown University / Watson Institute of International and Public Affairs, Nov. 2018, watson.brown.edu/costsofwar/costs/human/civilians/pakista ni.

Pearson-Merkowitz, Shanna. "Why Your Congressional Representative Isn't So Representative of You." *Pacific Standard*, The Social Justice Foundation, 17 Feb. 2014, psmag.com/news/congressional-representative-isnt-representative-73330.

Rogan, Tom. "Why the UFO Story Is Far More Interesting than You Think." *Washington Examiner*, Washington Examiner, 28 May 2019, www.washingtonexaminer.com/opinion/why-the-ufo-story-is-far-more-interesting-than-you-think.

Regan, Shawn. "5 Ways The Government Keeps Native Americans In Poverty." *Forbes*, Forbes Magazine, 13 Mar.

2014, www.forbes.com/sites/realspin/2014/03/13/5-ways-the-government-keeps-native-americans-in-poverty/#dcc98352c274.

"Revolving Door Prohibitions." National Conference of State Legislatures, National Conference of State Legislatures, 8 May 2019, http://www.ncsl.org/research/ethics/50-state-table-revolving-door-prohibitions.aspx

Shamsi, Hini. "Keeping Civilian Drone Deaths Secret Keeps Them Going." *American Civil Liberties Union*, Originally Published by The Washington Post, 15 Mar. 2019, www.aclu.org/blog/national-security/targeted-killing/keeping-civilian-drone-deaths-secret-keeps-them-going.

Shepard, Steven. "Gun Control Support Surges in Polls." *POLITICO*, 28 Feb. 2018, www.politico.com/story/2018/02/28/gun-control-polling-parkland-430099.

"Shroud of Secrecy around Civilian Deaths Masks Possible US War Crimes in Somalia." *Amnesty International*, Amnesty International, 20 Mar. 2019, www.amnesty.org/en/latest/news/2019/03/usa-somalia-shroud-of-secrecy-around-civilian-deaths-masks-possible-war-crimes/.

Strand, Mark. "Here's How to Reform Congress to Make It Actually Work." *Time*, Time, 30 Sept. 2016, time.com/4514717/congressional-reform/.

Tabakovic, Haris, and Thomas Wollmann. "Revolving Doors and Regulatory Capture." *VOX, CEPR Policy Portal*, The Centre for Economic Policy Research, 13 Sept. 2018, voxeu.org/article/revolving-doors-and-regulatory-capture.

Taibbi, Matt. "The Pentagon's Bottomless Money Pit." *Rolling Stone*, Rolling Stone, 17 Mar. 2019, www.rollingstone.com/politics/politics-features/pentagon-budget-mystery-807276/.

VHA Office of Mental Health. "Homeless Veterans." *Go to VA.gov*, 8 Mar. 2012, www.va.gov/HOMELESS/pit_count.asp.

Yglesias, Matthew. "Proportional Representation Could Save America." *Vox*, Vox, 15 Oct. 2018, www.vox.com/policy-and-politics/2018/10/15/17979210/proportional-representation-could-save-america.

Zeder, Jeri. "Elected vs. Appointed?" *Harvard Law Today*, Harvard Law Today, 1 July 2012, today.law.harvard.edu/book-review/in-new-book-shugerman-explores-the-history-of-judicial-selection-in-the-u-s/.

Economy And Wealth Inequality

Bandow, Doug. "Corporate Welfare Lives On and On." *The American Conservative*, The American Conservative, 29 Aug. 2018, www.theamericanconservative.com/articles/corporate-welfare-lives-on-and-on/.

Brunori, David. "Where Is The Outrage Over Corporate Welfare?" *Forbes*, Forbes Magazine, 14 Mar. 2014, www.forbes.com/sites/taxanalysts/2014/03/14/where-is-the-outrage-over-corporate-welfare/#eadce0227ddd.

CBS News. "Student Loan Debt Crisis: How Did We Get Here?" *CBS News*, CBS Interactive, 30 Apr. 2019, www.cbsnews.com/news/student-loan-debt-crisis-how-did-we-get-here/.

Chatzky, Andrew. "Inequality and Tax Rates: A Global Comparison." *Council on Foreign Relations*, Council on Foreign Relations, 12 Mar. 2019, www.cfr.org/backgrounder/inequality-and-tax-rates-global-comparison.

Cohan, William D. "How Wall Street's Bankers Stayed Out of Jail." *The Atlantic*, Atlantic Media Company, Sept. 2015, www.theatlantic.com/magazine/archive/2015/09/how-wall-streets-bankers-stayed-out-of-jail/399368/.

De Souza, Renata. "Governments Are Criminalizing Homeless People to Distract from Their Own Failures." *Amnesty International*, 2 Oct. 2017, www.amnesty.org/en/latest/news/2017/10/governments-are-criminalizing-homeless-people-to-distract-from-their-own-failures/.

Fagan, Susie. "5 Reasons We Need an Amendment to Say Corporations Aren't People." *American Promise*, American Promise, 19 Apr. 2019, www.americanpromise.net/5-reasons-we-need-an-amendment-to-say-corporations-arent-people/.

Friedman, Zack. "78% Of Workers Live Paycheck To Paycheck." *Forbes*, Forbes Magazine, 11 Jan. 2019, www.forbes.com/sites/zackfriedman/2019/01/11/live-paycheck-to-paycheck-government-shutdown/#911d524f10ba.

Friedman, Zack. "Student Loan Debt Statistics In 2019: A $1.5 Trillion Crisis." *Forbes*, Forbes Magazine, 25 Feb. 2019, www.forbes.com/sites/zackfriedman/2019/02/25/student-loan-debt-statistics-2019/#4ee897b5133f.

Greenfield, Kent. "Corporations Are People. Thank Goodness. - The Boston Globe." *The Boston Globe*, The Boston Globe, 2 Nov. 2018, www.bostonglobe.com/ideas/2018/11/02/corporations-are-people-thank-goodness/m5LK7UbeQFghj2K23tp99I/story.html.

Jickling, Mark. "Causes of the Financial Crisis ." *Congressional Research Service*, Federation of American Scientists, 9 Apr. 2010. fas.org

Labonte, Marc. "Systemically Important or 'Too Big to Fail' Financial Institutions." *Federation of American Scientists*, Congressional Research Service, 24 Sept. 2018, fas.org/sgp/crs/misc/R42150.pdf.

Lane, Rachel. "$15 An Hour: A Higher Wage, but Hardly a Living." *CBS News*, CBS Interactive, 15 Oct. 2018, www.cbsnews.com/news/15-an-hour-a-higher-wage-but-hardly-a-living/.

Lee, Adam. "Why We Should Tax the Churches." *Big Think*, Big Think, 22 Jan. 2012, bigthink.com/daylight-atheism/why-we-should-tax-the-churches.

Martin, Jena, and Karen Kunz. "Wall Street Regulations Need a Facelift, Not a Minor Dodd-Frank Makeover." *The Conversation*, The Conversation, 23 May 2018, theconversation.com/wall-street-regulations-need-a-facelift-not-a-minor-dodd-frank-makeover-97136.

Mattera, Phillip. "Subsidizing the Corporate One Percent: Subsidy Tracker 2.0 Reveals Big-Business Dominance of State and Local Development Incentives." *Good Jobs First*, Good Jobs First, Feb. 2014, www.goodjobsfirst.org/sites/default/files/docs/pdf/subsidizingthecorporateonepercent.pdf.

Morrissey, Monique, and Heidi Shierholz. "The SEC's 'Regulation Best Interest' Is in the Best Interest of Wall Street, Not Retirement Savers and Other Investors." *Economic Policy Institute*, Economic Policy Institute, 20 Apr. 2018, www.epi.org/blog/the-secs-regulation-best-interest-is-in-the-best-interest-of-wall-street-not-retirement-savers-and-other-investors/.

"New Rules Would Require Debt Collectors Have Proof You Actually Owe Money." *Consumer Reports*, Consumer Reports, 4 May 2018, www.consumerreports.org/consumerist/new-rules-would-require-debt-collectors-have-proof-you-actually-owe-money/.

Oman-Reagan, Michael. "It's Time for a Thriving
    Wage." *Medium*, Medium, 10 Mar. 2019,
    medium.com/@OmanReagan/its-time-for-a-thriving-wage-
    9d34f35c621e.

Prasad, Monica. "Actually, It Was Democrats Who Killed the
    70 Percent Tax." *The Agenda*, POLITICO, 5 Feb. 2019,
    www.politico.com/agenda/story/2019/02/05/democrats-70-
    percent-tax-rate-000879.

"Pre-Employment Inquiries and Arrest & Conviction." *U.S.
    Equal Employment Opportunity Commission*, U.S. Equal
    Employment Opportunity Commission, 2019,
    www.eeoc.gov/laws/practices/inquiries_arrest_conviction.c
    fm.

Prosperity Now. "Universal Basic Assets: The Tip of the
    Universal Basic Income Arrow." *Prosperity Now*,
    Prosperity Now, 24 Aug. 2018,
    prosperitynow.org/blog/universal-basic-assets-tip-
    universal-basic-income-arrow.

Robinson, Edward, and Omar Valdimarsson. "This Is Where
    Bad Bankers Go to Prison." *Bloomberg*, Bloomberg, 31
    Mar. 2015, www.bloomberg.com/news/features/2016-03-
    31/welcome-to-iceland-where-bad-bankers-go-to-prison.

Smith, S.E. "Burnout Is a Capitalism Problem, Not a Millennial
    One." *Talk Poverty*, Center for American Progress, 30 Jan.
    2019, talkpoverty.org/2019/01/30/burnout-capitalism-
    millennial/.

Stewart, Katherine. "How US Churches Exploit Tax Exemption
    to Promote Faith-Based Politics | Katherine Stewart." *The
    Guardian*, Guardian News and Media, 20 Nov. 2012,
    www.theguardian.com/commentisfree/2012/nov/20/us-
    churches-tax-exemption-faithbased-politics.

Totenberg, Nina. "When Did Companies Become People?
    Excavating The Legal Evolution." *NPR*, NPR, 28 July

2014, www.npr.org/2014/07/28/335288388/when-did-companies-become-people-excavating-the-legal-evolution.

Umez, Chidi, and Rebecca Pirius. "Barriers to Work: People with Criminal Records." *National Conference of State Legislatures*, National Conference of State Legislatures, 17 July 2018, www.ncsl.org/research/labor-and-employment/barriers-to-work-individuals-with-criminal-records.aspx.

Winkler, Adam. "'Corporations Are People' Is Built on an Incredible 19th-Century Lie." *The Atlantic*, Atlantic Media Company, 5 Mar. 2018, www.theatlantic.com/business/archive/2018/03/corporations-people-adam-winkler/554852/.

Wren-Lewis, Simon. "Why Top Rates of Income Tax Should Be Much Higher." *Social Europe*, Social Europe, 6 Feb. 2019, www.socialeurope.eu/top-rates-of-income-tax.